Eternal Romeo

Ricardo K. Petrillo
Claudio R. Petrillo
Silvia Knoploch

Copyright © 2010 Claudio R. Petrillo & Silvia Knoploch
All rights reserved.

ISBN: 1-4392-7024-4
ISBN-13: 9781439270240

OTHER BOOKS BY THE AUTHORS:

Eternal Bonds of Love – published May 2008

Poems for a Better World – published May 2009

Poems of Love – published October 2009

TABLE OF CONTENTS

Introduction	vii
Preface	xi
Rehearsals	1
Scene I - Lives	3
Scene II - Inspiration	7
Scene III - Detachment	9
Scene IV - Muse	11
Scene V - A Dream	13
Scene VI - Doubt	17
Act I – Hamilcar and Hannibal	19
Scene I - Phoenicia, third century BC	21
Scene II - Spain, some years later	27
Scene III - North Africa, many years later	49
Act II – Romeo and Juliet	53
Scene I - The streets of Verona, circa mid–fifteenth century	55
Scene II - At the Capulet's estate	65
Scene III - At the Capulet's estate, late at night	71
Scene IV - Romeo visits Friar Lawrence	75
Scene V - The wedding	81

Scene VI	- Duels	83
Scene VII	- The wedding night	87
Scene VIII	- Friar Lawrence's plan	91
Scene IX	- The tragedy	95

Act III – Life after Life   103

Scene I	- Lamentations	105
Scene II	- Realization	109
Scene III	- Resignation	113
Scene IV	- Remorse	117
Scene V	- Renewal	121
Scene VI	- Reviewing	125

Act IV – Romeo's Past Lives   133

Scene I	- Turor, Egypt, circa 67 BC	135
Intermission		139
Scene II	- Aton, Rome, circa 250 AD	141
Intermission		159
Scene III	- The Greek, Jerusalem, circa the tenth century AD	163

Act V – Planning the Future   169

Scene I	- Re-encountering Helena	171
Scene II	- Realizations	175
Scene III	- In the monastery	179
Scene IV	- Meeting Friar Lawrence again	183
Scene V	- The three visions	197
Scene VI	- Juliet	201

Act VI – Redemption   207

Scene I	- Two Blue Angels, Verona circa late seventeenth century	209
Scene II	- A dream	219

Closing curtains   223

INTRODUCTION

As an introduction to *Eternal Romeo*, I will succinctly recount our story, for those that have not read other books by Ricardo. Ricardo, our son, passed away at age twenty after a tragic fall at college. Inasmuch as this event could have destroyed our lives, marriage, and belief in God, it rather brought my husband and me closer together, gave our lives new meaning, and enhanced our spiritual beliefs and practices.

Healing from our unspeakable grief began as we received Ricardo's first message through his father, Claudio, nine months after Ricardo's passing. After several months of personal communications Ricardo told us we were going to write and publish a book in one year's time. *Eternal Bonds of Love* was written and published between July 2007 and July 2008. Their work continued intensely and in July 2009 *Poems for a Better World* was published, followed closely by *Poems of Love* in October 2009.

Eternal Romeo is the fourth such collaboration between Ricardo and his father. Ricardo "dictates" to his father through a process referred to as channeling. We believe we are eternal souls moving from one vibratory level to another during our process of growth and spiritual evolution. In between life experiences in flesh, our spirits are free in other dimensions where space and time do not exist. If we are open to explore these different realities with the aide of our "special senses" such as intuition and non-local mind skills (current scientific terminology), we may be able to access these different realms and communicate in various ways with our departed loved ones. After-death communication literature abounds with thousands of accounts of people interacting with those who have passed to the "other side" via dreams, hearing their voices (clairaudience), seeing them (clairvoyance), or obtaining signs that they are close to us (sometimes agreed upon before death).

Many doubt that we are indeed communicating with our son, that these messages and books are Claudio's way to work with his grief and that they are a product of his unconscious mind. We are certain that this is not the case as we live through this process. We may not be able to explain fully how it happens or how this is possible, but after writing four books in less than two years (with a fifth in progress), mainly in poetry form, when Claudio never wrote or published any works in his life, is proof enough for us. Furthermore, the details of the writing process are astounding. Claudio writes for about thirty minutes, three to five times per week; the previously written material is digitized by me and put away and not reviewed prior to the next "seating"; he will start the next page or chapter as if he had just read and reviewed the last section; there is no thought process, no pauses, no rewrites, it just "flows" seamlessly and effortlessly; he rarely makes a mistake or "scratches" what has been written. He has no idea of the whole, of what is to come next, or what the main idea or ideas are until the writing evolves.

While writing *Eternal Romeo* we often wondered what would happen to the characters next as we did not know details of Hannibal's story. As for Romeo and Juliet, although we knew the "plot" and ending of the legend, we were transfixed with the turn of events after their deaths, sensitized and joyous to imagine a happier ending to such an endearing but sad love story.

As Ricardo says in his preface, *Eternal Romeo* is a mixture of historic facts and fiction. Even though that is the case in this book, we believe that in "real" life, we live through similar experiences—that is, we "reap" in this life what we "sowed" in a past life. It explains to us why there are such inequalities amongst peoples all over the world with abundance in some countries and misery in others, why the tragedies we witness and experience ourselves and why different levels of knowledge and evolution exist even in our contemporary world.

Being scientists, as we are both doctors, we cannot accept that the Universe happened by chance and that everything and everyone in it also happened without any plan or intention. Although we do not believe in an anthropomorphic God, "sitting on a cloud" directing what will and will not happen to each of us, we believe in a Supreme Power, creator of all there is—creator, foremost, of the laws that govern the entire Universe, allowing both the material and non-material elements to evolve within these laws. As we know, the planet, its inhabitants, and all life forms in it have evolved through the billions of years that Earth has existed; we can study our past as a species and confirm the magnitude of changes that have occurred biologically, technologically, and spiritually through all ages and civilizations.

We are well aware of our past as primitive and violent beings, fighting each other for survival without any regard to any spiritual or moral values. Over time we have evolved, bettered ourselves; we started caring for each other and for the planet itself. What has determined these changes? Where do feelings of compassion, altruism, charity, and others like these come from? What has led to the changes in our genes? Where do feelings of love, spirituality, and religiosity originate from? Why would it matter or where would it contribute to our evolution and strength as a species?

Well, we certainly don't claim that Ricardo's books have all the explanations for these most intriguing questions. But we hope that the ideas and thoughts in them will lead some to enquire and search for answers that may bring a better understanding as to why we are here, where do we come from, and where will we go after the death of our bodies.

For those who, like us, have suffered a catastrophic loss, we say: our loved ones have not died, they are just a thought away, and they continue to be a part of our lives; so meditate, reflect, and open up your senses to let them in.

Silvia
August 2009

Preface

I feel blessed and privileged to be allowed to write this book through the hands of my father. The three previous books, *Eternal Bonds of Love*, *Poems for a Better World*, and *Poems of Love* seem to have been exercises in preparation for *Eternal Romeo*.

Through the daily practice of our communications, we have now reached a level in which I am able to pass all information and facts as if I was writing myself, with only minimal interference.

Eternal Romeo is an epic where historical facts and fiction merge in a kaleidoscope of feelings and emotions, and lives are all interconnected in the continuous process of rebirth.

From Hannibal to Romeo we would hope to project the evolution of a soul in the eternal pilgrimage toward our Divine Source.

Right and wrong can't be defined, success and failure are relative as the different realms and the different levels of vibration intertwine in a series of experiences aimed at the purification of the soul.

Centuries pass by when feelings are experienced and the acts of our consciousness work as a chisel shaping a rugged, common stone. From that stone a beautiful sculpture will arise one day as we proceed on a journey of inner transformation.

We also attempt to reveal in this book the effects that our acts inflict on others, directly and indirectly, and that we are ultimately accountable for their consequences. It is our sincere hope that through the humility of our poems, the messages are bright and clear.

It is the purpose of our work to dispel the idea that taking one's own life might be justified in some instances, whether for love, for honor, or in desperation. The processes that follow this act are always extremely painful as we all have within our souls the consciousness of the Divine, the miracle of Creation.

We are gods indeed; as we create and produce and as we understand ourselves more and more, we become greater contributors to all Creation.

Eternal Romeo as a book is not only an exercise for our next one, but a different approach to present history, a different light into us humans, not to justify our acts but to understand them, leading to the realization that who we are today reflects what we did yesterday, and who we will be tomorrow will reflect what we did today.

Romeo and Juliet, written in sublime poetry before, may the message be spread in our simple poems that life is sacred, divine, granted to us as a blessing, as our means to evolve, to expand our knowledge and spiritual potential so that one day we will all be part of a different world where greed, hatred, selfishness, and envy will be replaced by fraternity and love.

Ricardo
June 2009

Rehearsals

Scene I

Lives

Lives, so many
Thousands of lives
All intertwined
As if merging

Memories of lives
My lives?
Who knows, they blend
Become one, many…

The artist paints
With his words and poetry
The beauty, the drama
The passion, the violence

Lives, many lives
Thousands of lives we've had
To get to where we are
To get to whom we are

Never alone, however
As many other lives
Cross the paths of our lives
Many times, many…

Meeting in different circumstances
Exchanging roles
In the theater of our existences
We act, we play and learn

In the school of life
We come and go
Eternal students ever ascending
In our paths

The artist pauses, reflects
Allows his inspiration to take him
To different realities
Different realms

The real artist knows
That his hands are guided
And is humble, wise enough
To let them be taken to wherever they go

Like strokes of colors
Filling a white canvas
His words fill the white paper of the book
Like tears of love

The strokes of a pen
Guided by…who knows?
Would it be fiction?
Would it be reality?

What is the difference between fiction and reality?
Isn't the reality of fiction
Its own reality?

Then the artist travels
Without leaving home
He witnesses splendid views
Fantastic scenes
Always serene, into himself

A book, a play, a poem
His mind is at one with the world
As the poems acquire form and movement
What is behind the play?

Scene II

Inspiration

As the music played
Incessantly and irresponsibly
And the sounds reverberated
In the water of the Thames
The artist struggled in thoughts

How mundane, how shallow
Life appeared to be
How fictitious this apparent reality
How insane, insensate

In the depth of his heart
He knew, he could feel
The transient nature of all
And refused to be part of the scene

Detaching himself for a moment
From all, from the crowd
He felt himself floating
Above all, observing

The gondolas and boats
Carrying the characters
Holding masks to their faces
Exchanging frivolities and giggles

Their faces painted like masks
Suggested secrecy, sin
The air, heavy with lust
Pushed body against body

In a theater of desires
Emotionless, his gaze wandered
Registering all in his soul
Bringing memories, old memories
Of different times, different lives

A golden ray of light
Suddenly directed him to a valley
Very distant and serene
Where multicolored flowers
Created a carpet for lovers

There, two teenagers walked
Lost in the beauty of their love
Enchanted with all that surrounded them
Hearts merging in one

How innocent, how pure
Their true love captivated him so much
That he was taken along
And resting in the carpet of flowers
He sighed

Scene III
<u>Detachment</u>

Immersed in the wonder of his feelings
His mind empty of thoughts
The poet let himself float
Into the purity of his soul

The reality before him was open
But the duality of it all
Had vanished
He had freed himself of concepts
His heart was open as the sky

At a distance the teenagers
Danced in the flow of the breeze
Followed by a flock of birds
Singing hymns to true love

Was he awake? Dreaming?
His mind inquired
In quiet confusion he acquiesced
To allow all things to follow their course

The sky remained blue
The sun still warming his face
The scent of flowers
Inebriated his senses

The sound of music
Echoed in his ears
Music so angelic
Where was it coming from?

From a brook of crystalline waters
He drank to appease his thirst
And felt through all the confines of himself
The radiance of the Creator

Was he in Heaven?
Was this Paradise?
The answers, all around him
The realities for him to choose

Memories, old memories
Memories of different times
Memories of different lives
Began to carry his mind away

Space and time merged
With all stars in the sky
With the flowers and birds
The two lovers…

As he opened his eyes
The masks again, parading
The music, the crowd, all lust
The poet smiled, in joy

Scene IV
Muse

The world seemed to open
Its welcoming arms to the poet
As an invitation to thought
As to suggest creation

Amidst all the pomp
He felt alone
Imprisoned in his own body
Enslaved by his own mind

But now he'd had the vision
And the insight
That somewhere he had found
The meaning of peace and true love

How could he find it?
Where to look?
He looked around himself
To realize it was all darkness

Somehow he felt light
As he'd never felt before
The certainty of his vision
The serenity in his heart

Walking aimlessly with the wind
Drifting about the dirty streets
With the noise and the fetid smell of vice
He was light and pure again

His body moved easily
His mind empty of thoughts
And memories
He was now in search
Of his muse-Love!

Scene V

<u>A Dream</u>

Capitulating to the fatigue
Of body and mind
The poet fell into Morpheus' kingdom
Without resistance

A sudden luminosity, however
Seemed to indicate to him
A way, a path to follow
And held by diaphanous hands
He was shown a new world

Traveling at an amazing speed
He passed through times and places
Entire civilizations
Being born and extinguishing

He would clearly see and understand
The rise and fall of kings and emperors
Their transient glory and demise
As well as their past and next lives

He was given a glimpse
Of his own past experiences
Just enough to envision
What was ahead

Time again had no meaning
And people of different times
Interacted at the same level
And with him

The angelic hands
Guiding him confidently
Communicated peace and serenity
As his thoughts turned to himself

How little had he done so far
Member of a prosperous society
Favorite of the queen
Reaching for mediocrity

Shame invaded his core
As he now understood
He had something more to do
He needed to wake up to his real world

The hands were guiding him
Through stages of religions
And in what man
In its worst
Had transformed them

Scenes of the Inquisition
He had only heard of
Were parading before his eyes
And his senses were filled with horror

Kings and popes
In all their luxury and wealth
Sacrificing millions for their greed
The Crusades…

The birth of Islam
When Heaven sent Angel Gabriel
To present all its beauty
In poetry to Mohammed

The birth of Christianity
With all its martyrs
Spreading the message of love
And a different life

The life and death of Jesus
And His message
The consolidation of all messages
Of all times and cultures
Into a simple word – Love!

The poet had tears in his eyes
Overwhelmed by so much so fast
When at a distance he saw that same field
And the two lovers

Scene VI
Doubt

Awakened by that sudden call
The young poet still had in mind
Fresh and clear
The substance of his journey

How could he have seen
How could he have witnessed
So much in such a short time?
Was it all but a dream?

He felt he was no longer the same
And any acts, any thoughts
Brought to mind a fact, or two
Of the journey

Somehow he felt stronger
As if the information he received
Was already part of his memory
And he'd just finished receiving it

Some other side of him suggested
He disregard it all
Resuming life as before
Rejoining the court and the crowd

He got out of bed at once
And through the streets of London he walked
Observing all peoples
In the market and in the palace

They were familiar to him
More familiar than ever
He'd seen them before
He'd known them before

But now they seemed different to him
Enclosed in their own ignorance
They went about life
As if they were at a parade

So distracted they were with all around
They couldn't see inside themselves
So concerned with their need to have
They neglected their chance to be

As the poet walked away that day
Doubts in his mind evanescing
His strides took a confident tone
He had a job to do

ACT I

Hamilcar and Hannibal

Scene I

Phoenicia, circa third century BC

Following the first Punic war. A man, Hamilcar, talks to his eleven-year-old son, Hannibal, in a patio and garden of their house.

"My beloved son
In you I deposit all my hope
That one day our country
Will be restored to its rightful place

"Carthage in all her glory
Remains the pearl of the world
And despite our apparent submission
The force of the lion lives in us

"Envy and greed
Of our superior society
Has motivated our enemy
Barbarians in their Etruscan origin
To launch violence against us

"We were very close to victory
As I analyze it today
And rebuild our forces we will
To inflict upon them a definitive defeat

"Our past history and culture
Our superior engineering abilities
Our great sense as merchants
Will propel our rebirth

"My son, flesh of my flesh
I will pass unto you
The knowledge and skills of war
So that no general in Earth
Will ever be greater than you

"In these dark days when we all
Pay heavy tributes in gold and pride
I wish to pass unto you
All the hatred that I have

"Hardly contained in my chest
It makes my blood boil
At a mere thought of the Romans
At a simple word, a reminder

"Sleepless nights forever
Counting the stars in the sky
Waiting for the day that I'll witness
The Tiber filled with their blood

"Our first queen
Deceived she was in her love
Giving her life to the gods
As a sign to all generations

"Now we fall again
By virtue of our own neglect
To our eternal enemies
Just to rise for our vengeance

"Hatred my son, hatred
Be the force to move your life
In the direction of destruction
Extermination of their primitive lives

"The glory and knowledge of our ancestors
Will always be with you
As we begin at this moment
Our plan, our destiny…

"Surprise will be the strategy
Ingenuity and power the means
Courage and pride we will carry
While our hatred propels us

"Dream my son, dream
With the greatness of conquest
Their humiliation and shame
Enslaved by our superior race

"We should begin to train as we speak
Our elephants, our men
Our mighty cavalry
Our skilled engineers

"Our focus must be one
No distractions, no affairs
Other than our plan
Propelled by our hatred"

To young Hannibal these words
Had the effect of wild flames
Spreading over dry wood
As his body tensed up

He could sense his father's anguish
He could feel his pain
And in his child's heart
Hatred was being born

Hatred, a feeling new to him
Was taking over his body, his heart
He felt uneasy, anxious
Who could inflict upon his father
So much pain?

Father and child left the compound
From the hill they saw the sun
Setting its last rays
On their beloved city

Hamilcar continued:
"Beautiful Carthage
At your feet we come
To honor all your glory
And to praise your great tradition

"We ask the gods for wisdom
And courage
To make the right decisions
And to implement them with determination

"We swear before your majesty
To relentlessly pursue our enemies
Who have so dishonored you
Until the ultimate victory

"That our lives
And of all our generations
Never rest until
The Romans are destroyed"

Their eyes were petrified
Around them though not seen
Spirits of old warriors
Agitated the air into a wind
Their destinies were being sealed

Scene II

Spain, some years later

Hannibal speaks to his generals:

"Many years have passed
Since humiliation has fallen upon us
And heavy duties we still pay
For the luxury of our enemies

"However, our superior skills
In the art of trade and science
Have allowed us to rebuild
An ever-stronger Carthage

"From Carthage we have brought
Our best engineers and warriors
Our elephants and horses
And the wealth of our creativity

"But to Spain, we have also brought
Our indomitable spirit and honor
Our willingness to sacrifice
And above all we brought
Our hatred of Rome

"From Spain we will launch
An epic journey
To remain in the annals of history
As how we defeated Rome

"We have prepared for this time
For many long years
And now we have amassed together
The best that the world has seen

"We will traverse Europe
Doing what's thought impossible
Recruiting new warriors in our journey
All those with hatred toward Rome

"Carthage is alive
Wealthier and more beautiful than ever
And it is for her glory
That we declare war on Rome"

Hand over hand
In a gesture of unity
The generals saluted Hannibal
Their leader

His message was brought to all
Fifty thousand soldiers
Expressing their violent instinct
As a cloud of darkness
Lingered over their heads

Dark spirits of hatred
Violent, primitive in their stage
Guided the entire army
Through the confines of Europe

The spirit of Hamilcar
Who had drowned while riding an elephant
Was side by side with his son
Now a master in the art of war

The march was methodic and slow
With the elephants creating an odd picture
Terrifying the regions they passed by

After many weeks they arrived
To the land of the Gaul
Facing the waters of the Seine
As a gigantic barrier in their way

On the other side the Gaul
In large numbers and armed
Waiting for events to occur

"The voluminous water of the river
May pose a barrier to some"
Hannibal remarked
"But our superior science
And engineering
Will overcome it all

"The wood of the forest
Is our working material
And the ingenuity of our soldiers
Will create rafts

"They will be built with strength
Enough to bring our army
Men, horses, and elephants
To the other side"

To the amazement of the Gaul
Watching the strange scene
Of elephants floating in the waters
Of their sacred river
Hannibal started the crossing of the Seine

Not understanding it at all
The Gaul disbanded and ran
Away from the demi-gods
Opening the way to Hannibal

Darkness continued to increase
In the fertile grounds of Europe
As hatred was overcoming
Any sense of fraternity and peace

* * *

In just seven days
The world had witnessed
Something never conceived
Never imagined

Hannibal had his whole army
Not only cross the Seine in rafts
But win a free pass through Gaul country
Without spilling any blood

The feat was celebrated by all
Morale was as high as it could get
And singing along hymns of joy
And praise to Carthage
They marched

What motivated those souls
In their pursuits?
What moved them almost automatically
Toward violence and death?

Most eyes could see only one scene
Of warriors marching to war
But would fail to perceive
All interactions with different realms

As their feelings vibrated outward
A strong attraction was created
As an electromagnetic force
Bringing together hordes of warriors
From different times

In a wild interaction
Their sentiments merged
Creating a dark ball of violence
That rolled forward
Causing chaos and disorder

Still in a celebrating mood they were
When the first sight of the mountains
Paralyzed their march
Muting their chant

As images of powerful gods
The white peaks of the Alps
Commanded fear and respect

Hesitation and disbelief
Filled all of their hearts
Even the elephants balked
Before the majesty of nature

They had no fear of battle
Where they knew the enemy to fight
But the enemy they now faced
Was quiet, insurmountable

"Beyond these mountains"
Hannibal spoke
"Glory waits
Reward to the strong
Promise to the brave

"No man has ever crossed them
And no one expects us to
Brave man of Catharge
The glory will be with you"

* * *

The feeling of joy long gone
Having given space to desolation
Silence reigned in the camp
Almost submerged
By the white curtain of snow

Many had perished
Under the inclement force of winter
Horses, elephants, and men
As hope gradually disappeared

What strategies to use?
How can we utilize our skills
And great creativity
Against the forces of nature?

Hannibal, however, wouldn't balk
The fire of his hatred
Kept him warm and protected
Against this brutal enemy

Concerned with his heavy losses
But determined to proceed
He was looking for ways
Of encouraging his men

"Father, I invoke your soul
To come to our rescue
In this time of hopelessness
To bring us some light

"Many of our kind have perished
On behalf of our pride
In honor of Carthage
For the hatred of Romans

"Give me strength not to console
But to reach into their real core
Where their last resources reside
So that their hearts may be warmed
Their lives revived"

In the darkness of his tent
Hannibal noticed light approaching
And with his eyes semi-closed
He saw two images
Within the reach of his sword

At his left side
Projecting the beauty of her youth
Wearing the crown of her pride
Queen Dido appeared to smile

At his right side
Expressing the severity of the moment
And anguish in his voice
Hamilcar spoke:

"My beloved son, time has come
For you to reveal the nobility of your blood
And surprise the world
With the impossible

"You have been guided
By generations of warriors
Of many countries, many lands
With a common motive to fight
Hatred of Rome

"Now your time it is
To turn grief into strength
Losses into gains
Desperation into hope

"Fear not your destiny
As greatness you'll see
Trust your thoughts and your acts
Show the world what you can be"

Hamilcar's face was transfigured
As dark smoke discharged from his pores
Creating a dark screen
Blurring his image

The first queen of Carthage
Fixing her eyes deeply on Hannibal
Who now appeared asleep
Solemnly said:

"The gods of our nation
Who have granted us great wisdom
Have sent us here tonight
To bless you with their strength

"Centuries of glories and fame
Are now in your hands to claim
So avenge the honor of your queen
Avenge the humiliation of our people

"Strength you'll find inside
Every time you invoke our name
And your name will forever
Be remembered in glory

"Now you go, Hannibal
And take your men
One by one by the hand
Before being buried by inaction"

History cannot tell
And no one is known to know
How Hannibal got his strength
And pulled his army out of the Alps

* * *

As the rays of the sun
Dared again to warm their bones
Frozen by months of agony
Each and every man
Had a feeling of gratitude

They seemed refreshed
And regaining strength
As hope again
Appeared in their semblance

Even the animals appeared
Rejuvenated and strong
As the luscious fields of Italy
Welcomed their surprising arrival

Hannibal exalted
Despite the great loss
Of one half of his army
He rejoiced

"The spirits of our lineage
Have brought us here now
To avenge them
To avenge Carthage

"Despite our heavy losses
We still have our best brains
Our best generals
And each one of you
Soldiers of Carthage
Have the power of five Romans

"The element of surprise
Remains our main weapon
And throughout our march toward Rome
We'll allure many into joining us"

Indeed the odd and bizarre army
Led by elephants, horses, and men
Resembled children marching
Toward an exciting and innocent play

Many men they found in their way
Oppressed by the weight of Rome
Joined their army at once
Abandoning their families behind

Men in their blindness
Following their most primitive impulses
Leaning to violence
Leading to despair

If they would have at times
Stopped and reflected
They'd have a better chance to realize
How much harm, how much pain
They would have to endure

At a different vibratory level
But marching along with them
Hordes of warriors followed
Primitive, blinded by ignorance
Unaware of themselves

Above all, dark clouds appeared
To take the skies over Italy
Heralding storms
Darkness

"My brave generals
The moment of surprise is with us
Although I am quite certain
That Rome has been informed

"Our presence in these lands
Will provoke harsh response
And that will also play
To our advantage, to our benefit

"The Romans may amass legions
Many times greater than our army
So we will need to use our best ideas
In the science of war

"Let us march slowly
Regaining our strength and joy
Allowing new adhesions
Replenishing our energies

"As they react to our presence
With outrage and anger
We will surprise them with our weapons
And superior strategies"

* * *

Rome's reaction was swift
Surprised by the daring enemy
Confident in their power
Many legions were called into action

The golden eagle of pride
Symbolizing their growing empire
Would once more destroy
And subjugate their persistent enemy

As the two armies prepared for battle
From the confines of the underworld
Thousands of souls
Were being raised from darkness

The sense of impending violence
Like a giant magnet
Attracted those violent spirits
Primitive in their nature
Ignorant in their essence

In a scene unappreciated by most
They took sides
Through offenses and curses
Inciting their vilest reactions

Savoring the impending carnage
Leaders from phalanges of barbarians
Rejoiced in ecstasy
In anticipation of the battle

Pride, hatred, and greed
Had taken over the continent
Not leaving room for reason
Love or compassion

Going against the current of nature
Beings of all realms
Regressed to their most primitive origins
Rejecting their divine essence

With the speed of a thought
Hannibal initiated a surprise attack
Sending all elephants in front
And his skilled cavalry

Not expecting that approach
The Roman legionnaires
Were caught on their feet
And despite their skills and bravery
Were forced to retreat
Not before heavy losses

Hannibal had won
The first battle of a war
That would have no winners
As no wars ever have

Rejoicing with his generals and army
Despite heavy losses as well
Hannibal was energized

"We have come from Africa
To cross the ocean to Spain
To cross the continent to the mountains
To cross the Alps to Rome
To win the battle of our lives

"Now, Rome, here we go
With the strength of our hatred
With the support of our fathers and mothers
By you humiliated before

"Rome, oh Rome
It is time for you to kneel
In honor and respect
Of the son of Hamilcar

"Warriors of Carthage
Your bravery and skills
Are gifts given by our gods
Today celebrating with us

"Rome, oh Rome, kneel before us
Your masters to be
Our mercy you won't see
You will pay to your last man

"Brave warriors of Carthage
And all those with hatred of Rome
Our siege of the city will begin
And may be long
Until our flag flies throughout the world"

* * *

The following months
Were difficult and arduous
Recovering from bloody battle
Reassembling for the next

With his army now reduced
To one third of the original
And the loss of some mighty elephants
Hannibal needed help

He sent messengers to Carthage
Asking for reinforcements
More men, horses, and elephants
To sustain the final battles
The conquest of Rome

He would barely sleep
As the excitement of the impending victory
Kept his mind active all the time
Plans, ideas, strategies

The surrounding land
Devastated by war and abandonment
Couldn't produce enough
To nourish his hungry army

Missions were periodically sent
To regions sometimes far
Where they destroyed and ransacked
To obtain their needs

All was well and justified
As Hannibal was so close
To the greatest conquest
In the history of mankind

Pride and vanity
Were taking a toll
In the son of Hamilcar
Opening space for entities
Attracted by his feelings
To interfere with his thoughts

Vanity, daughter of pride
Growing on his ego
Like a tumor out of control
Hannibal the great…

The siege was indeed long
As disease began to spread
Affecting men and beast
Without regard

Hannibal, however, remained detached
In the illusory world
Where glory was his only choice
And fame his destiny

Rome, however, was far from defeated
Searching for the cause of her losses
Studying the root of the debacle
Feeling confident within her walls

Using Hannibal's own strategy
Decided a surprise attack
Sending Scipio Africanus
Directly to Carthage

Cold and methodic
General of many battles
Scipio Africanus was given
The best legions Rome had

Deprived from her best men
And her best generals
Carthage was vulnerable and weak
Falling into the hands of the Romans
With virtually no resistance

When the messenger arrived
Hannibal greeted him with surprise
Where the reinforcements?
Where the elephants?

The letter was brief and direct
Without room for misunderstanding
"Hasdrubal has been defeated
Reinforcements we can't provide
As Rome controls Carthage

"Abandon the lands of Italy
Return immediately without fight
Otherwise a high price
We're all destined to pay"

* * *

In the darkness of his incredulity
Influenced by a myriad of souls
With different purposes and goals
Hannibal remained detached

His arrogance so strong
And his pride overflowing
Prevented him from reasoning
Diminishing his great skills

His hatred ever growing
Would not let him concede defeat
To the hands of those
He was so close to conquering

With Hasdrubal, his brother, defeated
When attempting to bring reinforcements
Hannibal had no strength
To maintain the siege

Spain was again part of the Roman Empire
Carthage humiliated
His army weakened, reduced

"Father, I again invoke your presence
To help us in this tragic moment
When our mortal enemies
Seem again in control

"Our best brains remain with us
And again our skills and hatred
Should drive us to victory
And the recover of our city

"I invoke you as my father
And as the great warrior we know
To counsel us to decide
The next path to follow

"Defeat I will never concede
And I will fight to my last breath
Until Roman blood is spilled
And our beloved Carthage freed

"Your son and my brother
Failed in his attempt to help
And his requests to return home
I continue to receive

"But I'll surprise them in battle
As many times before
And once again regroup
To destroy their world"

Dark shadows danced
Around Hannibal
As if in a celebration
Of further doom

He was now completely surrounded
By souls of all kinds
Friends and foes
From different times

They had come from the darkness
Where they'd been
Attracted by his thoughts
His feelings and desires

Some seeking revenge
Some just thirsty for blood
Others without aim
All temporarily lost, drifting about

So much influence they all exerted
That Hannibal could no longer
Know if the thoughts were his
And with a tormented mind
He drank himself to sleep

Scene III

North Africa, many years later

That starry night of autumn
So calm to the naked eye
Failed to reveal the dark clouds
Emanating from Hannibal's mind

The Mediterranean calmly bathing the beaches
Of his previous safe haven
Left a taste of the sea, a taste of salt
In his tormented soul

Years had passed by
And images of the last battle
Remained as vivid and real
Corroding his strength

Lying down in the white sand
Eyes gazing through the sky
He followed the stars as a child
But his mind wouldn't allow

"If I'd just had more elephants"
Hannibal reminisced
"We could have surprised them again
And freed Carthage from their hands

"Banished for life from my homeland
Land of my father and ancestors
Like a common criminal
I still tried to regroup

"Ostracized by most
Fearful of reprisal from Rome
I've wandered from land to land
Drifting about homeless"

As Hannibal pondered
A macabre dance began
Around his resting body
Resembling a funeral

"With my hatred of Rome increasing"
He continued in tears
"And without means for revenge
My heart has been broken into pieces
In anguish and sorrow I've lived

"If I'd just had some more elephants
My fate would have been different
The world would have been revived
The honor of Carthage recovered

"Father, I invoke your presence
And of all builders of our land
To give me strength to rebuild an army
To die in war or win our honor

"This land is no longer safe
As my host has been pressured
By our mortal enemies
And I must again flee"

Hannibal curled up like a child
Sobbed in anguish and pain
While the dark shadows around him
Rejoiced in their frenetic dance

In the emptiness of the night
Time seemed to have stopped
As the stars, brighter than ever
Created a path with their lights

Taken by the hands
Of the dark spirits that surrounded him
Hannibal followed that path
That took him to his house

His figure now had partially merged
With some of the dark shadows
And his thoughts at times
The same

He had kept that powder with him
Only for the direst necessity
And guided by other minds
He held the pouch in his hands

"Hannibal the great I am
And the Romans I would have conquered
If I'd only had more elephants
If I'd only had more time!

"Hannibal the great you want, oh Rome
To show around like a trophy
But that I will not allow
That I will not concede"

He suddenly ingested all the poison
Imitating the act of Queen Dido
And with the harsh taste of victory
He laughed

He began to see all the shadows
And recognizing some as his enemies
Now laughing ever louder, ever louder
"*Coward,*" he heard, "*coward*"

He could barely move his arms
His legs were too heavy
His eyelids falling down
As more figures joined the dance

"*The great Hannibal
The great coward
Our revenge has come
Coward*"

ACT II

Romeo and Juliet

Scene I

The streets of Verona, circa mid–fifteenth century

The clear blue skies
And the freshness of a spring morning
Provided an apparently peaceful
Although vibrant feeling

Early season flowers painted the balconies
As people had begun taking to the streets
Wandering about their lives
In a quiet procession

Nowhere to be seen, however
Dark clouds of sorrow
Approached beautiful Verona
Attracted by their own people

As magnet attracting metal
Thoughts were calling spirits of discord
Hidden in the dark clouds of hatred
Strengthened by the opportunity of revenge

Two realities, two realms
Bringing together friends and foes
From different times
Different lives

Two families, two bloodlines
Several generations of hatred
Started no one knows how
Reaching a boiling point

In that fresh morning of spring
The most primitive instincts and emotions
Were in the air
Anger, pride, selfishness, and hatred

From a gesture, maybe a word
A full conflict was started
To the brandishing of the sword
Drawing the first blood of the day

The four servants that started it
Were joined by many more
In a senseless and violent combat
Where both realms merged

Montague and Capulet
Fighting for no apparent cause
Remnants of old times
In Catharge and Rome

Many scenes were unfolding
At the same time
At different realms
Different realities

At the streets and the piazza
Many more had adhered to the battle
Children, adults, the elderly
All carrying their share of passion

Through the battlefield
They emanated waves
Reflecting their worst instincts
Their hatred

Invisible to them
But by them perceived
A much larger crowd of warriors
Were fighting the same battle

Roman legionnaires at one side
Warriors from Carthage on the other
Practically blended with all
In the battlefield

From the heights a source of light
Brighter than one thousand suns
Projected its rays through the city
And with the rays, angels
Descending to the battlefield

Desperation and hope
Good and evil
War and peace
Intermingling in one larger reality

Seventeen centuries had passed
But the feelings had not changed
Many lives gone by
In the eternal circle of rebirths

The same leaders, same warriors
Different places, different outfits
But the spirits unchanged
As if time had no meaning

The luminous "angels," however
Although invisible to both realms
Were bringing hope to many hearts
That perhaps an end was in sight

Suddenly in a flash of a bright light
Riding a gallant black stallion
The prince of Verona arrived
Protected by two bright guides

As if struck by lightning
Paralyzing all their actions
The crowd at both realms
Became silent

The prince's voice was commanding
Peace once and forever
Between Montague and Capulet
Carthaginians and Romans
At the cost of their lives

The prince spoke with authority:
"For all these years we have
Witnessed your two families
Escalate your violence and hatred

"Old generations have passed
New generations have come
And with violence our streets you fill
But our tolerance has ended

"Montague and Capulet
Shall your blood be shed
By any act of violence
You'll pay with your lives or banishment

"The patriarchs are at fault
In perpetuating this senseless fight
Verona will stand above you
So end your quarrel and let peace be made"

In silence the crowd exited
Leaving in the cobblestones
Stains of blood
Remnants of their hatred

At the parallel realm
Warriors were seen retreating
As if to follow the prince's command
Unaware of their own reality

Arriving at a slow pace
Aloof, disconnected of all
Romeo Montague walked into the piazza
Meeting his cousin Benvolio he asked

"I see blood in the stones
Have we had a fight around?"

Inattentive and disinterested
After his cousin's explanation
He continued his remarks

"I have no interest in fights
I have no desire for duels
My heart pounds heavily
My mind wanders away

"Cousin, I've been having dreams
As real as your presence here
Dreams of wars and death
Dreams of love and life

"A sweet voice has been telling me
That time has arrived
For my destiny to be fulfilled
My twin soul I'll find
But then confusion and sorrow

"I am desperately in love
But my love she doesn't return
As she will spend her life
Her youth and beauty
Cloistered in contemplation"

As Romeo spoke
A luminous entity
Gently radiated fluidic rays
To limbic areas of his brain

Romeo was all emotion
Tears filling his eyes
He was in love
Indeed he believed

"Her name is Rosalind
From the house of Capulet
Her face I can barely see
My affect never returned"

The cousins walked away
Romeo deaf to any reasoning
Despondent with his apparent fate
Resigned to his misery

* * *

From the heights
A luminous entity descended
Whose beauty would blind our eyes
Dressed in splendorous brightness
Adorned with the crown of compassion

She approached Benvolio subtly
And extending her arms like wings
Placed her hand between his eyes

Immediately in the center of his brain
A small rounded area lit up
In a purple calming color
And he, as if guided, spoke

"Romeo, my cousin
Your words are heavy
And sink in the freshness of your heart
Resounding painfully

"I sense desperation has taken hold
Of a spirit always jovial
And ready to bring happiness
To whomever it meets

"Dreams I believe you're having
And in the dreams you seem to be living
Without listening to yourself
Without searching deep inside"

The luminous area was expanding
Inside Benvolio's brain
In a multicolor show
Of synapses

He continued:
"You claim to be desperately in love
With someone you've barely seen
And that your love is not returned
Rosalind, who is she?

"Your heart has opened for love
Ready for passion and desire
Sublimating all other facets of your life

"Follow the guidance of your dreams
Without fear or attachments
And they will forever guide you
To your real path and destiny

"The Capulet are receiving
The core of Verona tonight
In festivities they claim
Will be remembered for a generation

"Let us attend to them in disguise
So that you can observe your muse
Amongst many others
And compare

"And from there I believe
You'll unburden your heart
From the heaviness of now
And perhaps, only perhaps
You may return to your primal self"

As Romeo listened to these words
He had a vision of darkness, of death
And shaking his head in disbelief
He cried

Scene II

At the Capulet's estate

The Capulet's estate was all activity
Women walked hurriedly
With flowers and vases in their hands
Servants passing by with fruits and fowl

Girl Juliet observed this movement
Puzzled about the recent news
She'd just received
By her jubilant mother

"We were visited today
By a handsome nobleman
Who has honored us with his request
To take you as his wife

"The prince kinsman, Paris is his name
Man of virtue and fortune
As no other in Verona
You should feel so grateful"

Her mother's words resounded
So strange in her child's mind
So pure and innocent
Unaware of the mysteries of love

Disinterested she seemed
Somewhat fearful of the news
She let her fingers play
With her long dark hair

As guests began to arrive
She called her nurse for help
Somehow she did not know why
She sensed a special night

* * *

With masks covering their faces
Five well-dressed young men
Arrived at the festivities
Each one with his own hopes

Romeo felt his heart beating fast
And approaching Mercutio, his friend
Asked him to stop and return
Back where they belonged

"I've just had a thought, a premonition
That if we continue beyond these doors
Death will be looming to us
In all her cold and dark majesty"

Disregarding his thoughts completely
The young man compelled Romeo
To follow him in
As the dance was beginning

* * *

The musicians had begun to play
As the full moon extended
A bright silver path
Connecting earth and heaven

Angels from many galaxies
Descended in sublime procession
And with grace and harmony
Created a protective layer around
Unwelcoming darkness

As the guests arrived
They sensed the scent of love
Penetrating their core
And experienced peace

Guided by two angelical figures
Juliet entered the ballroom
Child, almost woman
Pure, excited

Visualizing her light
Expressing awe behind his mask
Romeo was guided to Juliet
As if by someone else's strides

As they began to dance
They were taken to the air
Floating around by the angels
As all time and space were no more

Their hands connected
Their bodies
Did not exist any longer
As the two souls in love
Reunited

There was no separation
Or identity
As they were one with each other
And the universe

There was no space for lust
Or desire
As pure love involved them
In a bubble of light and peace

They danced and danced
Without a word
As they recognized each other
In themselves

Detached from the rest
They disappeared
Exchanging every photon of energy
As their selfless act of love

Lives and lives were passing
As they smiled in their plenitude
And peace
When reason no longer mattered

In their ecstasy of love
The two children were being awakened
To their real selves
And in a natural move
Their lips touched

The music had stopped
But not for them
In their dream of reunion
Romeo lowered his mask
And they kissed again

* * *

"Lady Juliet, come now"
Her nurse arrived
"Time has run its course
And it is for us to retire
After a long night of festivities"

Protective of Juliet as if her mother
Nurse had observed intently
Juliet's cousin Thybault
Unhappily observing them dance

Suspicious of his feeling
She made herself closer
To hear him whisper within his teeth
"Romeo Montague, I'll make you pay for your insolence"

As the guests began to exit
And the musicians slowed the flow
Romeo and Juliet, hearts clenched
Parted their ways

Paralyzed by these events
Romeo stayed in hiding
Within the Capulet's estate
To be close to his muse

Her name he did not know
But he knew in the depth of his heart
That something definitive had happened
That would change his life forever

Scene III

<u>At the Capulet's estate, late at night</u>

As the clouds darkened the night
Hiding the light from the stars
And the moon wore a veil
Covering her face
Romeo refused to leave

His mind in turmoil
His heart galloping
He did not understand
What had happened to him

Her name he did not know
He knew her well
Where from
He wouldn't know

As his mind wandered
His eyes devised her figure
Beautifully sculpted in a balcony
And with delight he heard her voice

"Who are you and why
From nowhere you appeared
To steal my pure heart?

"Can I continue to live
Without knowing where you are
Who you are with
And if you care for me?

"I know I've known you before
Although my memory is short
But with you I felt whole
Near you I was complete

"A new flame in my heart exists
Burning my body from within
A flame so subtle and light
Burning me deliriously inside

"Can I live without knowing where you are?
Shall I sleep to find you in my dreams?
I know we've been together before
All I want is to be with you"

The girl's face reflected now
The light of the moon
That curiously had lifted her veil
In honor of pure love

Angels surrounding the place
Protecting them from any intrusion
Guided Romeo's steps
And in tears of happiness he sang

"The love of my life I've found
My lady, my girl, my life
My world was in turmoil
I was blind, deaf, and insensitive

"Now I see the light in your eyes
I hear the angels in your voice
My existence makes sense
To live in love for you

"Damsel of ten thousand secrets
I am under your spell
Keep me there forever
Let me be part of you

"Yes we've been together before
Many times, many lives
And tonight I found you again
And this time I can't let you go"

A kaleidoscope of colors and light
Involved the two lovers
As to seal their love
Protecting them from the world

They exchanged beautiful vows
Poems of love
Promises they made
Being together forever

Realizing who they were
Raised some fears in both
But their commitment of love
Would be for life or death

Scene IV

<u>Romeo visits Friar Lawrence</u>

As the first colors of the sun
Announced the arrival of a new day
Romeo walked away
Feeling light, feeling full

It seemed to Romeo
That his life had just begun
And the emptiness he had inside
Transformed into happiness

"Was I alive yesterday?"
He pondered in his thoughts
"Could I live without her?"
He asked himself smiling

Guided by his guardian angel
He walked without perceiving
Into the grounds of the church
As Friar Lawrence labored in his garden

"Awakened by this hour, Romeo
Could only mean that
You either couldn't sleep
Or haven't slept at all"
Greeted the friar

Always with a peaceful
And serene semblance
Friar Lawrence had a luminous aura
Felt by all he contacted

Patiently he listened with interest
As Romeo narrated his story
And his immense love for Juliet
Asking the friar to minister them
The sacred bonds of marriage

"Only a few days ago, I remember"
Friar Lawrence replied
"You came to tell me about your love
But a different damsel it was
That appeared to have your heart imprisoned

"Now you return to me
With even greater intensity
Surrendering your heart to Juliet
To whom would it belong tomorrow?"

Romeo was barely listening
To the wisdom of the friar
While dancing around him
In his innocent dance of love

Friar Lawrence felt as if a hand
Touching his forehead
Passed to him an idea
That could end years of violence

By marrying Romeo and Juliet
Montague and Capulet
Would have no other choice
But end their senseless hatred

Peace would return to Verona
And with it a better chance
To enlighten those hearts and souls
To fulfill his mission to his flock

* * *

Friar Lawrence had come to Earth with a task
Of bringing peace and love to his people
And a very special affection he had
For Juliet and Romeo

He had the gift
To communicate with angels
So he ardently prayed
For help and assistance

A familiar vision appeared to him
Guide of many instances
And to attend his prayers
With a sweet voice she spoke

"My good Friar Lawrence
Romeo and Juliet have not
Been brought together by chance
But by necessity

"They've been together
Many times before
Gradually solidifying
Their sincere bonds of love

"Like most souls in the planet
They've been in the circle of life
Many times falling
Just to stand back up

"This is their greatest trial
When they would be called to use
All that they've learned
Time after time, life after life

"They could become the pacifiers
Of large groups of spirits
That century after century
Have nurtured their violence and hatred

"My good friar, you have come
To your life to guide them
And to help them in this process
So they may succeed

"Their minds can't clearly think
Blinded by their flame of love
That has kept them together
Many times before

"They've been united as souls
So help them be united in flesh
And may the strength of their love
Overcome the hatred of most"

In a trance Friar Lawrence cried
The beauty of that image
Seen not by his eyes
Built an enormous emotion

He lay face down on the floor
Feeling the coldness of the stone
Penetrate his body to the bones
And realized the enormity of his task

Scene V

<u>The wedding</u>

The ceremony was simple
The twin souls united
One more time by the church
Representing God

Juliet's nurse, the only witness
To such a relevant act
That hopeful Friar Lawrence
Thought would unite their families

Protected by a fortress of light
The church allowed only angels
To bring their blessings to the couple
And fill their hearts with peace

"All was so perfect"
The friar thought
"And all is perfect
When love prevails

"I will present their love
To their families
And the purity of it
Will dispel all hatred of past"

Aware Friar Lawrence was not
That the hatred was long-standing
Centuries of violence and war
Hundreds of thousands of souls

Juliet and Romeo parted
Amongst vows of eternal love
Decided to meet in this fortnight
To consummate their vows

Scene VI

Duels

Romeo was light and serene
He loved his life and the world
He had no enemies but friends
He bore no hatred but love

Wandering by the streets of Verona
He saw Mercutio and his friends
In a heated argument with Thybault
And the Capulet

Light and smiling he approached
Bringing within all his peace
All his love
Immune to all hatred
Invulnerable

"For you I've been searching, Romeo"
Thybault yelled
"To avenge your insolence
To have you pay for your insult"

Shielded by his luminous love
Romeo could devise dark shadows
Inciting the two groups to violence
And humbly he replied

"Thybault, my friend
I love you as my family
I've never meant to insult you
Or any of your kind

"Forgive me if you can
For what you may have felt
I carry no will to fight
But friendship in my heart"

Romeo kneeled before Thybault
Gesturing forgiveness and peace
But Mercutio drew his sword
And angrily challenged Thybault

The two groups at either realm
Became agitated
As the two began to fight
For their honor

Trying to avoid bloodshed
Romeo jumped between the two
And surprised by his friend's act
Mercutio relaxed his guard

Everything was so fast and abrupt
Mercutio bleeding on the ground
In agony...

Trying to revive his friend
Who had exhaled his last breath
Romeo was confused, in despair
He was to blame, he was to fault
For his best friend's death

He was no longer thinking
As he looked at Thybault
Memories of times, oh memories
Scipius Africanus he saw

Forgotten hatred revived
The old warrior stood up
And with his friend's sword in his hand
Coldly, methodically
Began to destroy his worst enemy

The hordes of darkness applauded
The old warriors were back
With all their talents
And all their violence

The battle did not last long
Romeo's skills, to most unknown
Were overpowering to Thybault
Who, surprised and overwhelmed
Fell mortally wounded to the cold stone

With two lifeless bodies
Lying in the streets of Verona
Romeo woke up from his nightmare
"What have I done?"

Scene VII

The wedding night

"Banished for life!"
Romeo cried to Juliet
"How can I live without you?"
He whispered in desolation

To Juliet's room he had climbed
For what they expected to be
Their evening in paradise
The beginning of the rest of their lives

Juliet was confused
Mourning the death of her cousin
Immersed in a hostile environment
To her beloved husband

But her love was beyond
Any doubts, any suspicion
That Romeo was innocent
Of any violence, any aggression

They had given themselves
In body and soul to each other
And her love for him
Continued, if at all possible,
To grow

"We will overcome anything
That separates us
Time will appease feelings
And we will be together forever"
Juliet replied

Romeo continued
"What is the difference between
Ecstasy and sorrow?
What is the difference between
Happiness and desperation?

"Must we feel what we feel now?
From complete fulfillment
To total hopelessness?
Shall we react?
Or simply act?

"Oh, Juliet, this is
The happiest day of my life
And the saddest
And the feelings merge into one

"My mind cannot think
My thoughts are dispersed
Meaningless
Whereas my heart explodes

"Today is the first and the last
Day of my life
As I feel my life would be over
With the first rays of the sun

"But I also know now
That our love will never die
And in either this life or beyond
I will always be with you

"Let's not think of the future
As the future can bring us death
But in the present we shall live
And the present will live forever

"The moments we are living now
Are timeless, endless
So let's us not think
Of what to do, but be together
Now"

And so the lovers remained
With no more concerns
No more sorrow
Absorbed by each other

As the rooster announced
The dawn of a new day
In all its natural majesty
Romeo whispered in Juliet's ears

"Go see Friar Lawrence tomorrow
He will devise a way
For us to be soon reunited"
And departed

Scene VIII

<u>Friar Lawrence's plan</u>

Juliet awoke with her memories present
As if her reality had changed
And all she'd valued for years
Had become meaningless

Her mother came to her
Carrying some news
A decision by her father
The patriarch

In order to relieve all sadness
Brought by the murder of Thybault
He'd decided that a wedding
Would restore the family's happiness

The prince's kinsman Paris
A nobleman in all the sense
Possessing enviable fortune
Would take Juliet Capulet as his wife

The Capulet family was honored
In greeting Paris
With open arms
In this difficult times

So that happiness could be restored
The wedding would take place
In this next day of the week
With everyone's agreement

Numbed by this series of events
Juliet received the news
Gravely but serenely
Not a word, just a sigh

Without another thought
She left her home at once
Under the pretext of going for confession
Of all her sins
With Friar Lawrence

Juliet had no fear
As she remembered Romeo's words
And guided by her intuition
She was confident in her destiny

Friar Lawrence was waiting
As if informed of all events
And not expressing any surprise
He listened paternally to the girl

He knew what to do
As he had learned in a dream
And with the patience of a teacher
His plan he explained to Juliet

"Juliet, my girl
Flower in full bloom
You and Romeo belong to each other
In body and spirit

"You will take this vial I have
And as morning brings
The wedding preparations
You will drink all there is in it

"Slowly your eyelids
Will feel heavy
And you will fall
In comfortable deep sleep

"Your breathing will stop
Your skin will turn pale
You will have no reactions
All will think you've died

"As tradition and religious rules
You'll be brought to the family tomb
Where you will be waiting asleep
For Romeo, your husband, your love

"As you wake up I'll arrange
That you both are taken away
To a place you'll live your love
Until the day of return

"In that day you my child
And your beloved husband
Will reunite your families
As your love will replace hatred"

Juliet was listening to all
Expressionless, silent
As if guided by an angel
She held the vial close to her heart
And left

* * *

Pale as white marble
Beautiful and pure
Wearing her wedding gown
Juliet rested breathless

The family in disbelief
Wandered without aim
Grief and sorrow
Covered the Capulet's estate

The groom was disconsolate
Happiness having flown away
His ambition frustrated
How can anyone explain?

In the midst of almost chaos
Friar Lawrence called for a prayer
And then directed the parents
To take Juliet to their tomb

Juliet looked like an angel
In her restful sleep
Unaware of where she was

Scene IX

The tragedy

Romeo, in his exile
Was informed of the happenings
By his loyal servant
Not by Friar Lawrence's messenger

Forces of darkness
Enemies of past
Conspired to prevent
Friar Lawrence's plan to succeed

The monk sent by the friar
To inform Romeo of his plan
Was held in quarantine
Unable to leave town

Romeo had no hesitation
Never reflected, solely reacted
Returning without other thought
To Verona, to him forbidden

His heart pounding in his chest
He gradually weakened his defenses
Allowing for influences from those
Who only harm and violence sought

"My Juliet – dead!"
Hatred he didn't bear in his heart
But his acts were cold, automatic
His feelings temporarily numbed

He knew not what to do
But to see Juliet anyhow
And then perhaps
Some light on them might shine

As he approached the tomb
He was recognized by someone
Kinsman Paris, the groom
Who ordered him arrested

The old warrior was revived
One more time in Romeo
His strength and skills
With the sword and in battle
Emerged

Emotionless he was
As he methodically destroyed
That enemy of the time
Trespassing him with his sword

His mind now all open
To the voices of his old enemies
Chanting in unison his name
"Romeo, what to do next?"

He entered the tomb gravely
In sorrow and with great respect
To see the most beautiful figure
Resting on a marble stone

The candles revealed Juliet
Sleeping calmly in peace
As if dreaming with him, Romeo
All in white, his wife

There was no more time for thought
But in his mind scenes of a beach
In a very distant land
And a light indicating a path

Perhaps the path to follow
The only path
To end his life
To reunite with Juliet

His right hand was being guided
As he reached for his pouch
And grasped the poison
Purchased from the apothecary

Without hesitation he swallowed it all
And as he lay by Juliet's side
The voices were growing stronger
"Coward you are, coward!"

He did not quite understand
But he had heard them before
As they presaged much pain and suffering
Torments with no end

As he felt his body paralyzed
He regretted and repented
As the voices now echoed throughout
"Coward you still are
You die as a coward again"

As his breathing ceased
Romeo could see his inert body
And he noticed Juliet's now
Moving as waking up

He felt like screaming
But his body did not follow
He felt like embracing her
Kissing her with all his love

His pain ever growing
As was his desperation
In seeing Juliet confused
Cry over his dead body

"I am here, Juliet!"
She couldn't hear him
He saw the shades of darkness
Guiding Juliet's thoughts

He tried to stop them
But he couldn't
Still attached to his inert body
All he could do was observe

Weak in her desperation
Her hands guided, directed
Promising him eternal love
Juliet trespassed her heart

* * *

Friar Lawrence did not find
What he expected when he arrived
He was so full of hope
But sinister premonitions
Were tormenting his mind

He'd wished to achieve peace
Between the two families
Through the union
Of Romeo and Juliet

But all he found was
The lifeless bodies
Of a girl
And two young men

He kneeled before the bodies
And from the depths of his heart
He prayed

He prayed for protection
For the three spirits
Deprived of their earthly lives
By the hatred of others

He prayed deeply for help
For the couple who had
Taken their own lives
In desperation
And in the name of love

"They did not know better
At the time of their acts
But they were pure of heart
And their lives were guided by love"

So fervently he prayed
That in a trance he was taken away
Very far it seemed
Where he perceived a scene

Two young souls and himself
With angels of unbelievable brightness
Discussing their plans
And their future trials

In a fraction of time
He remembered, he recalled
His role and assignment
In helping the two souls

"You've come to guide them
And help them in their pursuits"
A sweet voice whispered
"But this is their trial
Not yours

"They must be tried with fire
And to fire they must respond
They have chosen their own paths
They will decide their fates"

Transported back to the tomb
He awoke all sweat and tears
Without a sense of failure
Or success

"Life will continue eternally"
The friar thought
"And many more trials
We'll all undergo

"There is no success or failure
Right or wrong
But successive experiences
That will bring other experiences"

Grateful for the insight he'd received
Friar Lawrence no longer cried
His steps were slow
His semblance serene
When he walked away from the tomb
And started consoling the two families

Enlightened by his vision
And protected by his guides
He narrated the entire story
To Montague and Capulet

At times he raised his eyes
As if lost in his thoughts
And he witnessed a scene
Not seen by the common eye

A large sphere of light
Was being created
Encircling them all
And the city of Verona

Golden rays changing to silver
And lapis-lazuli tones
Seemed to be showering on them
Creating small drops of light
As they touched each person

The two clans were in awe
Despite their enormous pain
They were experiencing something new
A sense of peace at last

Friar Lawrence seemed transfigured
His flock was all humble
And ready to follow his guidance

He exalted the love of their children
But knew that it was pain
That was about to transform them

He had achieved what he wished
Peace was to endure in Verona
Although he could not have envisioned
The extent of the sacrifice

ACT III

LIFE AFTER LIFE

"Darkness within darkness
The gateway to all understanding"

Lao Tse
Tao, 550 BC

Scene I

Lamentations (by Romeo)

"Why do I suffocate?
My throat burns as if lava
Was running through me
I can't move, I can't breathe

"Where is my Juliet?
The love of my existence
Why is all so dark?
Am I alive or have I fallen into hell?

"Oh, Juliet, you are in my mind
I need to move, to find you
But all I see is darkness
And attached to my body
I am imprisoned

"Why am I so lonely?
I scream in agony
But no one listens
Only the voices, again the voices

"Coward, they say, why am I a coward?
Who are they?
They sound so familiar
I've heard them before

"If I am dead
Why do I feel pain?
Why do I feel worm by worm
Slowly eating my flesh?

"I scream and my throat burns
I try to get away
From my own body
Just to be pulled back to it
Even more strongly

"Oh, Lord, creator of all light
Give me a glimpse of that light
So I may begin to understand
Am I guilty of love?

"My hands and feet
Are so cold
Whereas my throat and gut
Burn like volcanoes in activity

"Is this going to ever end?
How long have I been here?
Juliet, angel of my dreams
Come to my rescue, I beg you!

"Coward, they call me
Insult me, why?
Why do they sound so familiar?
Do I know them?

"If I could just fall asleep
And rest my mind for a time
I would most certainly understand
What is happening to me

"Maybe I am deep asleep
And this is only a dream
A nightmare indeed
But all feels so real!

"I need someone to talk to
Friar Lawrence, where are you?
You have consoled most of my sorrows
Be a lenitive to my suffering!

"But silence is all I hear
And the voices saying coward
And laughing
Familiar voices indeed

"Have I died or am I alive?
What is the difference between life and death?
Being and non-being?
I feel, therefore I am!

"I feel my bones as frozen icicles
Breaking and causing pain
I feel the bites of rats and bats
I suffer, I am

"Who am I at this time?
Am I Romeo, do I know?
I know little if anything
Confusion, chaos, turmoil

"I pray at this time of suffering
To the Divine Source of all things
Creator of the Universe
To have your love flow through me

"I thought one day I loved
That day is ever so distant
What have I done for love?

"In the stillness of my body
My mind is in turmoil
Thoughts, feelings, visions
Hallucinations them all

"I pray to you, our Source
That your peace would flow through me
So I can see you in me
From my darkness to your light"

Scene II

Realization

"Coward, you have done it again!"

"Voices, again voices
So familiar to me
Tell me who you are
Why do you talk to me?

"Time has passed
Time is no more
I've been here forever
And forever here I'll remain

"Could this be Dante's Inferno?
Could I have hope for a change?
Paralyzed I remain
In the darkness of my sins

"My body being corroded
Serving as nourishment to other lives
And I have sensed
Every bit of it!

"I'd think that repeated pain
Would eventually numb your senses
But senses I have not
And pain is as intense

"Suicide, what a coward act
Selfish in all regards
Coward indeed I am
Couldn't I live with a loss?

"I walk through the confines of myself
And realize my every act
Every single word, gesture
Centered in me

"Juliet, my love for you
Was the purest feeling I've ever had
And even that feeling was stained
As I expected return

"Our love was idyllic
A love ever growing even now
That in the misery of my remorse
I live with the putrefaction of my flesh

"I begin to understand now
The impermanence of all things
Ever changing, always renewing
At all realms of reality

"Life, so precious it is
In all forms
At all levels of energy
Life proceeds

"Within the darkness of my consciousness
I begin to realize the source
Of all my sufferings of now
And a small circle of light
Begins to shine in my soul

"I did not kill myself for you
My beloved Juliet
But for the fear of being without you
And now I lost you

"Coward, indeed I am
To destroy the precious gift
To me granted by the Creator
To serve others, not myself

"Oh, I am so weak
I feel so tired
My throat still burns
But I can now move my arms
And open them in a prayer

"Time, what is time
When all you have is darkness
Months, years, centuries have passed
But now I see some light

"I need to focus on that light
That promise of redemption
That source of new energy
Warmth, love

"The voices are so distant now
Voices, so familiar
I have heard them
Many times before
If I could just sleep!"

Scene III

<u>Resignation</u>

"Although my bones remain chilled
And the burning in my throat
Has not appeased
The sight of light
Suggests me some peace

"My wandering mind
Is less chaotic
At moments I feel
I begin to understand

"Restlessness moves me less
And my thoughts at times
Seem clearer
As I focus on the light

"Why should it be any different?
Have I done anything to deserve it?
It seems that my consciousness creates
The reality I am in now

"Consciousness, where would it lead me to?
My heart begins to open
And I feel less attached
Less disturbed by my body

"Dante's Inferno exists
Deep within ourselves
And as I think more deeply
And meditate
I realize where I am

"But who am I anyway
With such a short-lived memory
Of just a few years of life
When did Romeo become Romeo?

"I can move around more freely
And the worms cause less suffering
I am not the flesh they eat
And yet I am alive

"The voices, so distant now
Do not sound as threatening
Yet familiar
Anguished voices they are

"The fear they first inspired in me
Blinded me to their reality
Anguished voices, full of hatred
I fear you no more, return at your will

"My loneliness remains unchanged
But suffering it causes no more
I have used it to reflect
To ponder, to understand

"I move around the darkness
Following the circle of light
I feel lighter, freer
For the first time I smile

"Oh, Juliet, if you only knew
The discoveries I've made
The insights I've gained
I wish I could share all with you

"I see my body from a distance
Corroded, deformed, repugnant
That's what is left of Romeo
And for the second time I smile"

Scene IV

<u>Remorse</u>

"As the mud begins to settle
And the water clears
I have glimpses of myself
I experience all my acts

"As quickly as lightning
Thoughts turn into images
And my brief life
Is before me presented

"Very little really mattered
As most of my years
Were used in development
From childhood to adolescence

"Somehow I did not absorb
All the hatred that surrounded me
Acting almost as a pariah
In my own clan

"But a final trial I had
The reason for my coming to life
And at that critical time
I collapsed like a castle of cards
Blown by the wind of my past errors

"I feel a profound agony
Almost desperation
As the vision of my act
Returns to me in flashes

"Repeatedly I review my death
Over and over again
And at each time my throat
Burns down through my entire being

"What have I done?
Juliet, where are you now?
The entire Universe collapses
Leaving no place for me to be

"Oh God, our Divine Creator
Allow me to take Juliet's place
She has no fault of her own
Pure as a flower, innocent child

"Let me suffer again and again
The torments of my act
And her act, pure reaction
To my despicable selfishness

"Juliet, where are you?
May I be devoured by worms
Ten thousand times perhaps
So that your immaculate face
May be spared of sadness

"How inconsequent was I
In my selfish desperation
I was the cause of your suffering
Oh, I suffocate in affliction!

"Where was the violence inside me?
Why did I have to resort to violence?
And through my acts
Cause the deaths of Paris and Thybault?

"Oh, my mind explodes
As my remorse spills over
As pus from a deep boil
Revealing the fetid inside of my being

"But the thought of you, Juliet
Experiencing anything like this
Is indeed by far
The worst torment of all"

SCENE V

<u>Renewal</u>

"Blessed be the darkness
That surrounds me
Blessed be the suffering
That I now endure

"May I be given the strength
To use my pain and sorrow
As lenitive to others
And thus appease their pains

"Juliet, my love
If I could just have a glimpse
Of you right now
I'd be blessed for eternity

"At a distance I begin to see
The small circle of light
Growing in size and shape
As if approaching

"At the same time
Thin colorful rays of sun
Begin to penetrate the rocks
Shelter to my disgrace

"Like an answer to my prayers
They reach my inner self
And a sense of warmth
And peace invades me

"I have no reasons to smile
And no right for relief
But somehow I am being comforted
And given a strong sense of hope

"The rays of sun seem in effect
To be expanding my own insight
Into my own reality
Our true reality

"The agony that seemed eternal
Is gradually diminishing
As the circle of light expands
Confidently, so promising

"My feeling of remorse
Still strong
Does not prevent me anymore
To look at the light
Shining inside myself

"Who is here now?
I can feel someone's presence
Someone so pure, so bright
That the eyes of my consciousness
Are unable to see

"Reveal yourself to me
Oh angel of light
And help me purify the stains
Acquired through my acts

"Reveal yourself to me
And help me reveal myself
So I can begin to understand
Who I really am

"Fears? I no longer have any
And hope appears to be as hollow
Guide me, take me by the hand
In a journey of self-discovery

"Oh, blessed light that comforts me
Go and attend to Juliet
Use all your kindness and love
To bring her peace and joy

"Speak to me, sweet light
Reveal all your wisdom
So that I may begin
To retrace the paths of my destiny

"I know that somewhere
In the immensity of the Universe
A beautiful soul, twin of mine
Waits for me in my redemption

"Divine light
You bring me this certainty
And with that I gather strength
To take on any trials
Until in humility and virtue
Our twin souls reunite"

* * *

"I follow the pull of the light
Attracting me like a magnet
And gradually, slowly
After how long, who knows
I leave the tomb of my penances

"Again I see the sky
Flowers, trees, and mountains
Darkness left behind
With the remains of the past

"Everything is so bright
The colors of sharpness
Not witnessed by me before
Are felt with all my senses

"The scent of moist leaves
And the perfume of flowers
Inebriates my spirit
For so long intoxicated
By the poison of my acts

"As the light continues to pull me
Without resisting I follow
Floating aimlessly in the air
Like a feather in the wind

"My thoughts are disintegrating
Stillness controls my mind
No more sorrow or regrets
For the first time I fall asleep"

Scene VI

<u>Reviewing</u>

"Oh how have I longed for sleep!
One single moment without a thought
With the mind resting
After how long? Who knows…

"The sense of sleeping was conscious
And I was aware of it all
But rest I have very little
How could I rest after all?

"Self-pity I had no more
Fully cognizant of my deeds
I was grateful for the light
And for being out of my prison

"As time was no longer a factor
And days, months, and years
No longer mattered
I had a sense of relief

"What mattered was inside
Resting somewhere within
Now asking to be revealed
Anxious to be expressed

"Letting my whole being float
Effortlessly I deeply inhaled
The fresh air of Truth
Exhaling the resistant shadows of pride

"Through agitated waters I sailed
In search of myself
Looking for the root of my acts
The source of my disgrace

"From high in the sky
Brought by the Eastern wind
A voice echoed in my ears
Thunderous and sublime"

*"Your journey has just begun
As many times in the past
A journey in which your past
Present and future are one*

*"A journey very familiar
You've been through it many times
But at each time
A new lesson, a new opportunity"*

"The voice silenced with a roar
Of a large wave
Throwing me overboard
Into a solitary beach"

* * *

"The silvery shine of a full moon
Illuminated my path across the beach
So familiar it was
I'd walked that path before

"Soon I was able to devise
Lying on the sand
Eyes fixated on the stars
Someone I knew so well

"My whole being trembled
As I penetrated that mind
And in a timeless way
Read all his thoughts

"I was indeed scrutinizing
My own thoughts
My own mind
And terrified I was!

"My worst symptoms recurred
As the burning in my throat
Was so intense
That in reaction I withdrew

"Compelled to continue
By what force I don't know
I saw legions of darkness
Surrounding my old self

"Hannibal once I was
My memories were so clear
How could so much violence and hatred
Inhabit just one human being?

"My fear was dissipating
As I had much to learn
I realized those thoughts of hatred
Attracted more violence from darkness

"Old enemies, murdered violently
By a man without principles
With only his hatred and pride
Guiding his acts

"I felt inside me
All that coldness
And I shivered
Once again ashamed

"As the hordes of enemies
Virtually took control of his ideas
I followed my old form
To the critical end

"*Coward,*" they all shouted
"*You will soon be gone
Having to face us all
We're waiting for you*"

"Revisiting that scene was so hard
But something inside me
Kept me strong
There was a purpose after all

"As I again witnessed
My first coward suicide
I was led to the hordes
Who delighted with my suffering

"Hannibal the Great, I pondered
How little of you
Lives now in me
Where was all hatred gone?

"Familiar scenes I continued to see
Many so recent in my memory
The prison, the suffering, the confinement
The worms, rats, and worse

"All enemies feeding off by the hatred
Torturing that spirit that blind
Would not release the mind
From the bonds of pride

" *'If I just had more elephants'*
Loud laughter exploding
How could I have tolerated all that?
All so distant
All so close

"Hannibal, you still live in me
In some moments of violence
Where, blind and without reason
I let you control my acts

"I fall on my knees in prayer
Giving thanks for the wisdom
To allow us opportunities
To continue to grow, to improve

Eternal Romeo

"I still hold great remorse
For my acts of recent past
But I know now and forever
That hatred I no longer harbor
In my heart

"Hannibal, I will let you go
And remain but in my memories
To guide my future deeds
In all my trials to be

"My throat burned immensely
I felt like passing out
The familiar voices more distant
How can I repay you all?"

* * *

"I walked aimlessly through the desert
Solitary and empty-minded
No directions, no fixed plans
Without intention to arrive

"The movement brought me purpose
And thinking weakened my mind
So I contemplated from a distance
The disastrous results of my acts

"The suffering and all put aside
As it reflected only in the self
I watched the turmoil of people
Perpetuating the hatred I spread

"Carthaginians and Romans
Hundred of legions at either side
Continuing their battles and conflicts
At all realms of life

"That reality was sobering
And my mind
So constantly fixed on the self
Had to find a new paradigm

"How many generations
Could I have influenced
To sustain such blind hatred?

"Like a parade in the sky
Uncountable souls appeared
Were they friends or foes?
I could barely tell

"For certain they were no demons
But live souls like me
And I wished them
No personal harm

"I realized that account was still open
And had to be paid one day
And for that I would have to prepare"

ACT IV

Romeo's Past Lives

Scene I

Turor, Egypt, circa 67 BC.

"Transported with the speed of a thought
I found myself by the Nile River
In an impoverished hut
Next to a squalid boy

"Once again I recognized myself in him
As his thoughts became mine
His feelings and mine merging
My memories were revived

"Turor I was
Then eight years of age
Very hard of breathing
Malnourished in appearance

"The mother had passed at his birth
The father laboring in the fields
Had left Isis, his older sister
A second mother to him

"Feeling his severe dyspnea
And bouts of unstoppable coughing
I bent myself in weakness
As energy I had none

"Born with a breathing disorder
Turor was ill from inception
Unable to thrive
And to grow

"Food he could barely take
As it regurgitated back
Unwelcomed by his body
Burning with each morsel swallowed

"Isis was his angel
With her black eyes and long hair
She was his mother, sister, and goddess
The only reason for him to live

"She would at times chew his food
To make it easier for him to swallow
And sing beautiful songs
That would calm his despair

"Oh, how much I loved her
I thought, as the feeling revived in me

"In my most anguished moments
When wheezing and gasping for air
Made me wish for the peace of death
She would rest my head in her bosom
And slowly I would breathe again

"At the age of eight I could
No longer walk by myself
Bound to a bed of leaves
That Isis had built for me

"Each leaf of a color
Exhaling a pleasant scent
'To help you breath better'
She would say
'To make you soon get well'

"And I believed her with all my heart
And despite all my sufferings
I smiled with the light of each day
I felt happy to be alive

"As the illness progressed
I felt I was gradually detaching
From that squalid body
But my spirit was strong

"Love had entered my life
As love was all I had
All I ever experienced
In those short-lived years

"Sheltered from the world by my illness
Not many people I'd encountered
As Isis was my bread
Water and air!

"Her voice was still echoing in my ears
Always serene, nourishing
And the warmth of her arms
Always ready to embrace me

"Suddenly I realized
I was happy!

"As the first touches of death
Began to involve my being
Isis never ceased to smile
Although some tears I remember

"She took the mystery out of that moment
As if a natural transition
Was about to occur
And confident, although somewhat reluctantly
I was set free

"I felt light and serene
I could breathe and move
I was free from the prison
I had set for myself

"How grateful I am for that life
Where all I had was love
A love that would bind us forever
Ever growing, ever expanding

"With Isis I want to be
For the rest of my experiences
Oh, I know it so well now
What have I done to you, Juliet?"

Intermission

"I am again taken to a desert
Where I can contemplate
From all sides, horizons
And at the center of all
Myself

"Horizons from past lives
Horizons of lives to come
And in the silence of the desert
My reality of now

"In the solitude of the desert
Where the wind whistles
Over dunes of sand
My eyes are filled with tears

"There is no other place
I want to be but here
Where the magic of nature
May reveal the mysteries
And the beauty of life

"I let my thoughts be blown
Aimlessly by the wind
And as my mind rested still
My inner vision expands

"From darkness all lights arise
As my vision begins to reveal
Something of me, yet unknown
Something to be discovered

"The desert and I become one
And the stars, the wind
All the lives and thoughts
I am open!

"I open myself to insight
And the entire universe
All stars and galaxies of all times
Past, present, and future
Begin communicating with me

"Suddenly I am one with all
And a great sense of peace
Never experienced before
I feel through my whole being"

Scene II

Aton, Rome, circa 250 AD

"The winds were blowing north-east
In the direction of Rome
And despite my reluctance
I was taken away
From my serene solitude

"I floated by familiar places
Cities and countries of Africa
And some nostalgia I confess
Temporarily took hold of me

"The Mediterranean could be seen
And felt with all its majesty
Kissing the coasts of Africa
Refreshing it from its torrid heat

"Alexandria with its beauty and wisdom
Toward the Middle East
Where Carthage was no more
Flattened by the fury of the Romans

"I kept nevertheless
No shade of hatred in my heart
When arriving at Ostia
The gateway to the Roman Empire

"The busy port was familiar
As hundreds of ships
Being loaded, unloaded
Brought and took people away

"Like a magnet pulling me
I was attracted to a group
Seemingly arriving from Africa
Mostly young men
In the prime of their strength

"Aton was his name
Sixteen years old
Chained to others alike
Slaves to be sold in the market

"Strong body for his age
Aton watched everything
Expressionless
No anger in his eyes, no hatred

"As I witnessed these scenes
And recognized myself in Aton
Confusion filled my mind
Who am I?

"The burning in my throat
Continued to be so real
As to distinguish
My current self

"Romeo is dead, I ponder
Or is he?
I felt alive as ever
Witnessing my past as present

"I had so many questions still
But a force kept on pulling me
Toward the group of slaves
Toward Aton

"I remembered growing up in freedom
As my parents were prosperous
And provided me with their love

"I felt complete as a child
Advancing my studies
In philosophy and the arts
I had everything I needed

"Although governed by Romans
We could maintain our beliefs
Have our spiritual practices
Following centuries of tradition
And wisdom

"But lady fortune turned her face
And smiled to the other side
Bringing shame and destruction
To our family, our lineage

"Paralyzed in disbelief
I was taken as a slave
In payment for a debt someone claimed
Against my father in disgrace

"Together we were one last time
A family to be divided for life
By greed, treachery and a system
That represented I couldn't say what

"We held our hands together
As many, many times before
And silently elevated our hearts
To the Absolute force of Nature

"I asked for strength
To survive apart from them
And for them never to succumb
To their own sorrows

"I remembered seeing a light
Descending from infinite space
From many different directions
Filling my entire being with power

"I am immortal, I thought
And so are they
Nothing can bring us apart
As our spirits will always
Remain together!"

* * *

"The market place in Ostia
Was crowded with people
From all over the world
And beyond the Roman Empire

"We were lined up to be seen
And examined by patricians
With different needs for labor
Different in all senses

"Plinius Tulius was an honorable man
Beyond the surface
Of the patrician pride
A calculated kindness could be felt in him

"He approached me soft-spoken
Inquiring about my life
My skills, my education
He seemed indeed personable

"A connection was quickly made
As we talked about life
Without fear or reservation
I felt respected

"Plinius asked me if I would
Want to join his household
As a servant, employee
As if I had a choice

"A sense of happiness invaded me
Or relief I would say
Toward Rome I was going
Without hatred or fear
Fascinating, Rome

"Unchained and with the promise of freedom
I arrived at Plinius' estate
Exulting but humble
And silently thanked Ra*
For His protection

---

* Ra, sun-god of the Egyptians

"As Plinius made the introductions
My eyes wandered away
To the patio and garden
Where a most beautiful pearl
Tended to the flowers

"Her eyes and mine crossed
As lightening had stricken us both
I was paralyzed, blind, and deaf
To everything else around

"In that fraction of a moment
We contemplated eternity
A marvelous journey without limits
Where space and time disappeared"

* * *

"A moment, a fraction of time
Would change our lives forever
Infinite, eternally present
Two souls reuniting

"The angels rejoiced
As the two hearts vibrated
In unison
Two souls, one destiny

"Helena was her name
Daughter of Plinius and Priscilla
Where had I met her before?
What was going to be of me now?

"With my mind in disarray
And my heart smiling
I was taken to my quarters
To my new life

"The Tulius family was kind
And generous to all
And to the servants
They never called us slaves

"There was a promise of freedom
But for most purposes
Freedom we indeed enjoyed
In the hours granted to ourselves

"My duties were many
From heavy household chores
Transporting the family to places
To teaching the children of servants

"Helena was constantly in my mind
If not in my sight
I would delight in listening
Her sing beautiful melodies

"The sound of her voice
Inebriated my heart
And the scent of her perfume
Would make me stumble

"Weekly on Friday evenings
As the sunset announced
The conclusion of another day
I'd take them to a ride

"After some five miles away
The Via Apia would lead us
To a modest small village
Surrounded by fertile fields

"We would leave the carriage
And continue by foot
For a mile, perhaps more
'Til we met a familiar group

"Kinder people I had seldom met
They appeared to carry the peace
Of the Universe
In their hearts

"We separated at that point
As more people continued to come
And disappeared as they entered
Into a place inside the rocks

"I was left to meditate
Under the stars and the moon
How lucky and fortunate I was
To be with Helena at times

"I knew in the depth of my heart
That she felt the same for me
As we both knew so well
The distance separating us

"I did not need much more
Than these few moments
Where our eyes rested open
Reflecting each other

"And our hearts beating
Rhythmically run by our love
As if our souls had been freed
To unite in oneness with God

"In those moments I waited
Dreams of happiness
Visions of love
Were as real as the sky

"I knew, oh, I knew so well
They were dreams to be kept that way
Visions beyond my eyes
Yet, I was content"

* * *

"Days and nights passed by me
And I didn't perceive
Idyllic life of mine
Serving Helena

"Love, so great it was
Calm and serene
Without the fire of passion
And the torment of possession

"Some days when the sun was bright
We walked around the garden
Helena reading me stories about
The one she called
Her Savior

"Beautiful stories of love
And great compassion for all
And lessons of divine beauty
Poems of great wisdom

"Helena and Priscilla were Christians
A sect harshly persecuted
By Rome and the Romans
For reasons nobody knew

"Some nights when the full moon
Extended a path of light
As to suggest us to follow
We talked about our lives

"I was able to tell her my life
That despite the pain of separation
Forced upon me and my family
I had found peace at her side

"Our love was sublime, untold
Strong within the two of us
Always present, with no expectations
Impossible though always there

"Helena's faith was strong
And that gave her a radiance
That could be seen
From far away

"Slave I was indeed
And slave I'll remain forever
Even after being granted freedom
Slave to my love for Helena

"Days, months, years passed by
And our lives were flowing like a river
Running serene and confident
In the direction of the sea

"Helena's commitment to help
The poor and the desperate
The sick and the needy
Grew strong as her heart

"I was no longer only there
To bring her to sites and places
But in my heart I believed
We were partners for life

"More and more people attended
The meetings of Friday evenings
Even with the threat of punishment
By the cruel law of the time

"The people were kind
Honest, sincere
A great sense of solidarity
With themselves and all

"Until the day all things changed
When subtly and without warning
Pervasive and extending a black mantle
Over the people of Rome
The plague arrived"

* * *

"In the beginning it was a rumor
Whispered in the streets
But soon the rumor grew
Into a dark, sad reality

"Brought by oriental travelers
It arrived from different sources
Somber sign of death
Inflicting pain and sorrow

"The first victims were the poor
Living at the periphery of Rome
But soon it invaded most homes
Uninvited, pervasive

"Stains that spread through the skin
Quickly changing into ulcers
Distorting faces
Destroying families

"The gods must have been punishing Rome
As Jupiter's anger spread
Not sparing anyone
Patrician or slave

"The mighty Roman Empire trembled
Shaken by an enemy
That would destroy all legions
Penetrate all defenses

"A desperate attempt to run away
Incited many of the rich
To abandon all they had
In order to leave Rome

"But the mighty enemy had
Long-reaching arms
Not sparing anyone
From its reach

"Helena and Priscilla
Joined the group to which they belonged
In providing care and comfort
To the afflicted and the suffering

"Days and nights with no rest
Cleansing wounds
Soothing sores and praying together
Bringing light in the midst of misery

"As the black plague spread
Corpses piled up everywhere
And I brought many in the wagon
To give them dignified burials

"In the beginning a few
But quickly there were so many
That our effort seemed futile
With no end to be seen

"The burial sites for Christians
Could no longer accommodate
For so many corpses
As we incessantly dug
To build more spaces

"Amongst all the misery and desperation
Helena maintained her radiance
As an angel in mission of love
Sent from heaven to earth

"We worked side by side to exhaustion
And when our eyes met
Drawn by the strength of our love
We shared with each other our feelings

"Oh, how happy we were
In the midst of so much misery
We whispered each other
Words from our hearts

"Poems buried for so long
Allowed to the surface
In the midst of desperation
Our sublime love shining high
In the devastation of death

"Panic-stricken Rome was
There was no one family spared
The temples of marble were full
Of corpses of the high priests

"The Christians nonetheless
Appeared determined and serene
As if internally their faith
Provided strength and peace

"We continued our work
For how long I couldn't say
As for us time had stopped
We were one in heart and spirit"

* * *

"When two spirits, two souls
Vibrate in perfect harmony
Time and space are dissolved
In the plenitude of love

"Facts and events of the moment
Even the most disastrous
Become mere happenings
Part of the flow of the Universe

"Love is so powerful
It transcends all things
As our love transcended ourselves
When we distributed it to others

"Plinius' household was dismantled
As Priscilla perished away
But Helena remained pure
Without a sole complaint

"With happiness and suffering
Side by side
We were running with the flow of life
Resigned with what we were given each day

*"Have faith in the way things are
Accept the world as it is"*
We heard in our daily gatherings
Of faith, prayer, and fraternity

"All persecutions had ended
And for a time I believed
We were all brothers and sisters
Born from a common source

Eternal Romeo

"We continued to bring bodies
To lay in a common grave
Without distinction of creed, race, or social status
All returning to that same source

"When Helena held my hand that day
My entire being trembled
As if all had collapsed
Her words were simple and calm

"I could see a twinge of blood
As she coughed
And although she was still radiant
Her outer skin was pale

"All her efforts, all her work
Must have weakened her pure body
And without sadness or fear
I realized, she was consoling me

"As a child, I could not accept
I had gone through this before
But now it was beyond conception
Beyond what I could understand

"Helena continued to smile
And reveal all her faith
Suggesting that our love would endure
And live forever in us

"Her voice, so angelical
Her words, poems of love
As she sang": *'Life is eternal
And eternal our love shall remain'*

"She announced visions of light
Beautiful scenes where peace reigned
But when she heard Priscilla calling her
I knew it was the end

"She kept her eyes open
Looking at me with her love
Trying to give me the strength
And the hope of our near reunion

"I closed her eyes in desperation
With a frightening cold in my heart
As voices I began to hear
Familiar voices I know

"I was expressionless, cold
My mind was so empty
But the voices…
They were telling me something I knew

"Without Helena I had no purpose
The voices said
It would be easy to join her
In all her glory

"Disconnected from my own reality
I rested my body next to hers
As my hands heavy and strong
Forced the blade into my heart"

Intermission

"Darkness within darkness
Is there a glimpse of hope?
I wander aimlessly
From existence to existence
Just to fall back into darkness

"But from darkness all lights arise
As I watch my past
My present I understand
And the future I can contemplate

"There is no hiding, no refuge
Where I can escape my consciousness
But the need, the urge
To reconnect to my essence

"Oh, divine universal wisdom
Shed some light in my poor spirit
Guide my steps and my choices
Show me the path to redemption

"Oh, Absolute Source
From where all things are created
Extend to me your compassion
Allow me to redeem my failures

"Recurrently I keep destroying
The gift of life to me granted
Always in selfishness
Always in vain

"I begin to see the light again
As I begin to understand
The power of my own creation
The consequences of my own acts

"Oh Helena, Iris, oh Juliet
Will I ever see you again?
I know I am far away
But time and distance
What are they?

"From Hannibal to Aton
Many centuries have passed
Hatred I no longer harbor
There may indeed be some hope

"One cannot however escape
The consequences of one's acts
Destroying what nature grants
As an opportunity to grow

"A scar remains deep in me
Asking to be removed
And what in flesh you destroy
In flesh you'll redeem"

* * *

"My journey continues steadily
To the very depths of myself
Where I am yet to find solace
But awareness is arising

"Small, insignificant as I am
I've seem to have created havoc
In many beings
In many lives of past

"In my solitude of now
The voices are sometimes present
Voices of hatred
Voices of fear

"My vision expands
As I open myself to insight
And I begin to see
How everything is so simple

"The wisdom of the great laws
That controls all universes
The common source of all beings
All worlds, galaxies…

"Getting lost in my thoughts
I travel to that time
In which I saw myself
Designing my next steps

"The constant pain
Of my last act of violence
The sense of guilt
The self-inflicted scars

"As an architect I began
Step by step
Building every block, every facet
Of my next opportunity
My next trial

"Remorse, pain and solitude
Unable to see my Helena
Helped to clear my inner vision
Creating colorful rays of hope

"Without the primitive senses
Or the concepts of time and space
I realized for the first time
The impermanence of all things

"A sense of oneness with all
Invaded my inner self
Giving me the courage to decide
On the painful course to follow"

Scene III

The Greek, Jerusalem, circa the tenth century AD

"My memories guide my journey
As I am heavily drawn
To the Middle East of the world
Where old Jerusalem waits

"I sense the violent vibrations
From inside and outside her walls
Where warriors, Romans, and Carthaginians
Renew their vows of hatred

"Wearing different outfits
Fighting for different causes
The same spirits remain
Attached to their circle of desires

"As I enter the city
Like a magnet I am attracted
To this cachectic beggar
People call 'the Greek'

"Deformed body and legs
Paralyzed by early disease
He sits in a low wooden cart
Attempting to move by the streets

"Doubts I have none
As my memories pass by me
Poor, crippled, and lame
'The Greek' became my name

Eternal Romeo

"Born from Christian parents
In a land run by Muslims
Disease approached me early in life
Paralyzing me except my arms

"My mother, so devoted
Taught me everything I knew
And soon I was reading the Gospel
As well as history, philosophy

"My lame body did not allow
For any gainful work
So a street beggar I'd become
In my wheeled wagon, in the streets
My home

"Stories I would tell the children
Who happily always came
To bring some happiness to my life
'The Greek' they said, my name"

*"He knows what nobody does
Stories, incredible tales
His mind is sane and wise
A Greek philosopher he must have been"*

"My life was to learn and teach
In a land where knowledge was free
And Jews, Christians, and Muslims
Lived and learned side by side

"Knowledge and faith were respected
And despite my physical handicaps
I believed I had enough
And contributed in helping someone

"But times had changed in those days
As violence and fear could be felt
And the threat of destruction
Extended its dark clouds
Over old Jerusalem"

* * *

"They came from the North
Thousands of knights with a mission
To take Jerusalem
From the hands of Muslims

"Moved mainly by ambition
Their violence was beyond belief
And they wore the cross
Symbolizing the One
Who turned the other cheek

"Almost barbarians they were
As they understood knowledge as heretic
Fanatics one might seem to think
Ambitious most of all

"Stories of the horrendous crimes
Were widespread in Jerusalem
They had eaten the flesh
Of those they'd killed in combat

"Understand I could not
As we worshipped the same God
And his Son who'd given his life
As an act of love to all

"The siege had now been long
As we were isolated inside
And food had been saved
For those who would fight in battle

"Resigned with my fate
I continued to talk and teach
The children of Jerusalem
The messages of love I knew

"Children in great fear
Jews, Christians, and Muslims
Children of the same God
All coming from the same source

"We sang songs of times
When the warm rays of the sun
Brought us messages of hope
And men could live in harmony

"Many attacks came to the north wall
But from the east they entered the city
To bring destruction, violence
Death

"From my wooden cart I witnessed
Crimes of such cruelty
And disregard for human life
Jerusalem was bleeding again

"No one was safe
Regardless of creed, age, or gender
And the cruelty exceeded
Any stories I'd ever read

"When I saw his face
Staring in my eyes he was
I had a sense of compassion
He did not know what he was doing

"He walked in my direction
With heavy steps holding his sword
His bloody uniform revealing
The cross

"I was calm and serene
I looked him in the eyes
He hesitated
Not a word we pronounced

"Around him I could see
Deformed images perhaps demons
Inciting him to more violence
Intoxicated by the blood

"He finally capitulated to them
And with almost disinterest
He forced his sword into my chest
Ending the life of 'the Greek'"

ACT V

Planning the Future

Scene I

Re-encountering Helena

"Oh, I see it so well now
And I feel as it happens
The doors of a prison opening up
To let the rays of sun come in

"From my lame body
That so well had served my needs
Light as a butterfly
I rose to the light

"Greeting me was Helena
Wearing a diaphanous violet light
Taking me by the hand
As a long-lost child

"Somehow I looked back
To old Jerusalem
All covered in darkness and blood
And in sorrow I cried

"How could I feel happiness
In the midst of such horror?
Slowly we were lifted away
From those scenes and tragedies"

"I've been waiting for you
It's been a while perhaps
But together again we may
Continue our journeys of growth"

Eternal Romeo

"Helena's voice had the sweetness
Of the purest nectar and honey
And despite my still-fresh memories
I felt serene and in peace

"We reached a peaceful settlement
With beautiful gardens and fountains
Where we washed off some harsh memories
And drank the water of hope

"There was so much to be said
There was so much to be heard
And in that way we remained
The two of us as if we were one

"I was able for the first time
To see my deeds of past
Not as violence but as learning
Evolutionary stages to be conquered

"I understood well enough
That all of those that I'd influenced
Directly or not toward hatred
Would remain in my account

"Noble Helena, my true love
Where does your love for me come from?
Reveal this secret to me if you could
Do you see what I have done?

"I must show you I can bring some peace
To the souls I've stirred to violence
And would still have the strength and the courage
To survive the worst adversity"

"I would with you forever be"
Helena's words caressed my ears
"To give you strength to help you indeed
To overcome all challenges you'll have

"Twin souls traveling eternally
From world to world
From life to life
Together our destiny is"

"How much time we spent
I may not be able to say
But little by little a plan
For our return was being born"

Scene II

Realizations

"To us free will is granted
To think, to create and act
From a thought, an image
Our creation, a fact

"The laws of the Universe
We have written in our hearts
No one may claim ignorance
We become what we build

"In our infinite climb to Heaven
Many journeys, many existences
We are blessed with opportunities
In the eternal school of life

"Our future plans were being drawn
As an architect designs
The blueprint for a house
Its structure and details

"We received input from many
Much wiser than ourselves
But ambitious we remained
So confident, ever so confident

"Without the cover of the flesh
Without the presence of desires
We saw everything so clear
We both aimed for the sky

"Yes, excitement there was
Faith in our strengths and hopes
Confidence that our love would win
Any battles and adversities

"We prayed together for strength
As we would indeed require
To overcome all obstacles
That we needed to succeed

"With many we discussed our plans
Measured the pros and cons
Shall we be less ambitious?
Shall we be less bold?

"Many counselors we listened to
But the decision was ours
And the decision was made
Together we would be invincible!

"With our hearts full of hope
We bathed in the river of forgetfulness
For a new chance of redemption
And in Verona we would meet"

* * *

"Days and nights pass by me
And I can't perceive them
Dark and light alternate
As my mind travels away

"Alone again, eternally alone
I find myself amidst my thoughts
I am reluctant to understand
As my heart struggles, my mind…

"Why is it, Romeo
That after being given all you wanted
You've again stumbled and fallen?

"My memories of past
So alive in me at this time
Remembrances of forms and names
That quickly arise and disappear

"Forms and names now gone
The essence remains strong
In a spirit eager to grow
In a soul searching for light

"I have known love, and how
Love has guided
And misguided my acts
For love I have lived and died

"With desperation no longer harboring
In my heart
A calm feeling of resignation settles
And an inner voice whispers:
Wait

"The universe appears to me
In the very palm of my hand
Disorganized and out of control
As the inner voice repeats:
Wait

"A kaleidoscope of colors
Covers my inner vision
And again and again
My past lives run by me

"Why is it repeating?
Have I missed anything?
I've gone from hatred to compassion
From pride to humility

"And love I've found, and how
And for love I've died
Have I?

"The voices return to my mind
As to remind me of something
Something I know
Coward!

"The voices I fear no more
Myself I fear no more
As I let my thoughts swim away
With the waves of the vast ocean

"I board the boat of my destiny
And let it take me where it wants
Trusting completely the Divine
I fall in deep sleep again"

Scene III

In the monastery

"I wake up to the sound of birds
Singing in harmony a song
Suggesting freedom and peace
Where am I?

"I rest in a simple bed
In a small room with white walls
A small table in a corner
Some flowers and a jar of water

"A large open window
Welcomes the warm sun
To bring life in
And comfort to my soul

"How long have I been sleeping?
The answers do not come
As I sit in my bed
Looking around for clues

"I take a few steps to the door
And looking outside I realize
That I am in a monastery
With a central garden

"I see monks walking calmly around
Attending to many in other rooms
Like myself, I think
Lost and without reference

"For a moment I feel dizzy
And my throat begins to burn
So I take some sips of water
And to my bed return to rest

"I feel like myself, Romeo Montague
Although weak and tired
And with a knowledge of past
Memories of different lives

"I close my eyes and let
The warmth of the sun
Penetrate my being
And raising my thoughts to the heights
I pray!

"I give thanks for the gift of life
That despite my attempts to destroy it
Continues offering me new chances
New opportunities to take

"I give thanks for the gift
Of remembering my past deeds
Allowing me to understand
Who I really am

"I feel blessed for the grace
Of having loved as I have
With such intensity and devotion
My sweet Juliet, where would you be now?

"I don't feel in my heart
The right to ask for anything
With faith in the way things are
I trust what is to come

"A sense of peace and serenity
Takes control of my whole being
I feel light and levitating
I feel whole for the first time"

Scene IV

<u>Meeting Friar Lawrence again</u>

"Romeo, my son, open your eyes
Take a deep breath and feel
The scent of spring flowers
Greeting you in your return"

"The voice so familiar and warm
Brought so much happiness to my heart
In true joy I opened my arms to him
Friar Lawrence, is that you?

"We embraced for some time
As tears ran through my eyes
I was not alone after all
After so long"

"You have never been alone"
Friar Lawrence remarked
"As the divine justice always provides
The help one requires

"We have been with you
All this time
Guiding your steps and thoughts
As much as we're allowed

"Despite your thoughtless act
You have many friends who love you
Whom in the past you've helped
And comforted in their afflictions

"They have all sent their prayers
And thoughts of love to you
Allowing us to this point
Where we are together again"

"Friar Lawrence looked the same
But around him I perceived a light
So subtle almost imperceptible
Giving him a sublime radiance

"I had so many questions
And didn't know how to start
Until I realized that he could
Read all the questions in my mind

"In silence I remained
And in awe
To be with Friar Lawrence again
I was so grateful"

"Romeo, my son, you've been trailing
A long winding road
Where you've risen many times
Just to fall down again

"That's the road that most choose
In their paths to the heights
But despite many falls
You have grown, progressed

"You've reviewed some lives
By the grace of the Creator
Whose mercy and kindness
Allows us to learn

"Therefore meditate
And find your truth within
With the knowledge that you now possess
Return to your primal self

"Romeo, your life wasn't wasted
As no life ever is
Despite your selfish act
Of violence against yourself

"Many of the souls that for centuries
In the darkness of hatred have lived
In part influenced by Hannibal
Were there in Verona at that time

"Romans and Carthaginians of old
Carrying their hatred along
At times as Christians and Muslims
Crusaders in the depths of darkness

"Astonished and confused by your love
The love of Romeo and Juliet
And your violent, senseless deaths
They rested their hatred aside

"The divine wisdom
Using the tragic situation
Sent its angels to help
In that moment of agony and pain

"Oh pain, greatest teacher
Taming the most recalcitrant souls
Divine tool of change
Divine tool of love

"Capulet and Montague
Romans and Carthaginians
Both in flesh and spirit
Reconciled in your names

"Juliet and Romeo
A symbol you've become
Of love to the last consequences
Brought peace and love to so many

"Despite your foolish acts
You've brought an almost end
To generations in war
And for that I've returned"

* * *

"Friar Lawrence seemed
To be able to read through me
All my feelings, doubts, and questions
Naked I was before him

"I had a sense of trust
So much trust in him
That comfortable I felt
In all my transparency

"No need to hide my feelings
No sense in being defensive
No effort to pretend to be
Someone other than me

"How much time, I realized
We spend in trying to be
Someone other than ourselves
To please someone else?

"I was beginning to realize
Who I really was in essence
The self instead of the ego
And I liked it"

"You wonder what is of Juliet"
Friar Lawrence added
Reading through the core of my heart
"And if together you will be

*"Much time has passed
If measured in earthly years
Since you both foolishly
Gave an end to your lives*

*"Just to realize your lives
Never ended but went on
What you perceived to be
Your eternal hell*

*"Since I myself have discarded
The ailing, old body of a friar
To come to this lighter realm
I've been close to the two of you*

*"What is time anyway
When eternity is before us?
And space, what is it?
Is there beginning and end?*

"Juliet is well as of now
And longing for you she remains
Though she knows by now, understands
That the act that you'd thought would reunite you
A great barrier became

"Noble spirit she is indeed
Yet far from being a saint
Weakened by fear and emotion
Acted without restraint

"Quickly she understood her fall
And, suffering, no one she blamed
Resigned with her chosen fate
She prayed for life and strength

"Her prayers were heard by many
As every sincere prayer is
And light and strength she received
In return for all she had done

"Nothing is forgotten in time
As the universe keeps memory
The many that she had helped
Prayed for her in return

"Her prayers then were raised for you
Entangled in sorrow, confusion
Until slowly, gradually
The light you began to see

"Romeo, you are now recovering
From your own deeds of past
Attended in this monastery
By the goodness of monks

"With you I will remain
As guide, give you advice
But again the choice is yours
Amongst the many paths to follow"

* * *

"Friar Lawrence left me
Promising to return often
As I felt tired and fatigued
In need of rest

"I was being tended and cared
By the dedicated monks
Always pleasant and caring
What did I do to deserve it?

"I had learned so much
About life and myself
And that made me realize
How much more there was to be learned

"Juliet, it makes me so happy
To know that you are well
How do I long to see you
To share the much that I've learned

"From time to time I still feel
The burning in my throat
As reminder of the poison
Testament to my selfishness

"Juliet I can now feel
A glimpse of hope in my heart
That soon we'll be together
We'll no longer be apart

"I understand painfully now
That what separates us
Is the distance of our acts
Oh, how much I repent!

"No punishment I receive
Will ever be harsh enough
No sentence too long
If together we will be

"I pray for light and strength
To let me find the way
To make me choose the path
To redemption

"Harm to many I've caused
But I've also sown seeds of love
Hatred I no longer harbor
In my solitary heart

"I feel somehow, I know
That I will have to return
As many times as needed
Until I find the light"

* * *

"It was a bright, sunny morning
The birds, celebrating the arrival of spring
Sang excited hymns to nature
Friar Lawrence and I
Walked through the garden"

"Look at these red roses, Romeo
How pure and beautiful
Each one unique in their beauty
Unaware of it

"Protected by sharp thorns
They exhale a sweet perfume
Revealing their essence
Without malice
For all to feel and see

"Each flower in the garden
Keeps a secret of its own
Nevertheless they all display
Their best for all to see"

"As Friar Lawrence spoke
I began to feel an urge to act
Uneasiness inside
Discomfort within myself

"I knew his words were wise
And directed to my needs
And even though I did not understand them
I was being affected

Eternal Romeo 191

"A great sense of urgency I felt
When we stopped under a tree
That graciously offered us shelter
And protection from the warm sun"

"You and Juliet ended your lives
Before the time given to you
And the vital energy remains
Latent to be exhausted

"In the Universe nothing is wasted
And the agitation and anxiety you feel
Urges you to complete your cycle
Out of respect of nature

"I am here to help you
To decide, to make choices
Understanding nature's laws
And the law of action and reaction

"We'll always have our free will
Within the framework of the law
Therefore, Romeo, reflect
And decide wisely your path"

"Friar Lawrence held my hands
And before my eyes I saw
Roads going in all directions
Some straight, some winding

"I wanted to reach for the sky
To redeem myself at once
But I'd done that before
Just to fall back again

"Inviting me to relax
Friar Lawrence said a prayer
And petals of all colors
Softly began falling from above"

* * *

"I started entering
The realm of my possibilities
As someone entering a maze
Not knowing its end

"I knew I'd be helped
At any time I needed
Without judgment
Without prejudice

"However I'd come to realize
That I was my severest judge
As I needed to decide wisely
Without haste to redeem my faults

"On one hand I was grateful
To be allowed to decide my fate
On the other hand I feared
I might lack the strength to the task

"As I navigated the realms of possibilities
I understood the difficulties we face
Once in flesh again, without memory
Relying in our senses and desires

"I knew I'd receive help
As we always do
As long as we open up to it
And remain sensitive, alert

"I had to complete the cycle
By me interrupted abruptly
And to unload the heaviness
Accumulated by my senseless act

"Little by little I cleared my mind
And a sense of relief
Invaded my soul
A blueprint of a plan I had"

* * *

"Relieved I was
And resigned
To enter a new chapter
To enter a new stage

"I did not question my decision
I carried no doubts in my heart
That after the next stage
Many more would come

"I knew I carried the knowledge
And suffering had made me realize
What were the paths to redemption
What was the road to ascent

"The monks were very kind
And helpful with information
And Friar Lawrence's visits
Were always comforts to me

"But sadness and nostalgia
Were gradually building in my heart
As if half of myself was missing
Juliet, you are always in my mind

"I walked around the beautiful country
That surrounded the monastery
Drifting as a wave on the ocean
Lost in the depths of my thoughts

"Despite the harshness of my choice
For the next stage in the flesh
Where my spirit would be a prisoner
Unable to express, to flourish
I was anxious for my trial to start

"I could no longer stand
My separation from Juliet
And although I understood why
And believed to be resigned
I was suffering…

"Friar Lawrence brought me hope
His goodness and wisdom
Were soothing for my broken heart
Living the miseries of its own acts"

*"Your choice is courageous and wise
It will open up new doors
New blessings will arrive
For the foundations of a new building"*

*"His words were liniment for my wounds
Still so fresh and bleeding
Still so painful
And I listened"*

*"From the many paths
Toward the light of our Creator
We choose those we need
The ones we can ride*

*"As you complete the next stage
New roads will open up
Offering you new alternatives
New ways to progress*

*"So, Romeo, stand up
And face yourself in the mirror
Reflecting the image of your essence
Understand it without attachment
And you'll succeed!"*

Scene V

The three visions

"As my time to return approached
I was growing more anxious
Frequently suffering the burning
And the pain of before

"My confidence was shaken
Fear was building up
Inside my heart
Throughout my mind

"I had failed many times before
When the veil of forgetfulness
Allowed the passions of the moment
To overcome the sense of my soul

"I prayed in those difficult times
To gain strength
To find purpose
To continue in my planned task

"It was in one moment
Of meditation and prayer
That from the heights she appeared
In a vision or a dream

"Iris was as I remembered
Wearing a purple mantle
Surrounded by a subtle
And bright light

"Her face expressed the love
That she had given to me
In times that I needed
In times long gone

"Her presence brought me back
To Egypt and the river Nile
When my frail existence
Was filled with love and peace

"Oh, how much I loved Iris
She was my saint
My protector
My sister, mother, and father

"She seemed to have let go of herself
To be at one with me
With my needs
With my life

"With Iris I'd learned to love
A love pure though possessive
Where I received much
And gave little

"I realized in her semblance
That she still suffered
With my present pain
With my fears and doubts

"She had come to bring me peace
Comfort and confidence in myself
To let me know that at anytime
She'd be there to hold my hands

"Her light changed in intensity and hue
As did her face and her hair
A light blue gown she was now wearing
Helena, how I remember you!

"Helena's smile was full
And penetrated my entire being
Bringing me happiness
I felt so light

"With Helena I'd learned
That love was also giving
Without expecting anything
In return

"Our love was immense
And we kept it in our hearts
As precious pearls
Hidden at the bottom of the ocean

"Love so unselfish
Without the stains of passion
Helena had come to bring me
Her faith in my chosen path

"My vision was blurred by clouds
As a prelude to a storm
When in the blinding brightness of lightening
The image of Juliet took form

"She was beautiful and pale
Her lips red as a rose
Partly open as to say
I love you!

"She wore a long white gown
To contrast with her long black hair
Falling over her breasts
Pointing to her heart

"Her heart I could almost see
As droplets of blood
Silently spilled over
Through the self-inflicted wound

"Oh Juliet, my sweet Juliet
With you I learned to love
With all the passion of the flesh
And all the intensity of my spirit

"I feel my own wounds reopen
For being the source of your pain
For having being so weak
And selfish

"Juliet had come to me
To share her love
To share her life
In happiness or in sorrow"

Scene VI

Juliet

"*R*omeo, my love, only God knows
How much I've longed for this moment
Come, Romeo, come to me
The divine mercy has answered my prayers"

"Paralyzed by Juliet's voice
Speechless, expressionless I was
Unable to grasp its meaning
Unable to realize its truth

"For so long I was living
Through different levels of reality
Where time and space blended
In a turmoil of feelings and emotions

"Moving through perceptions and dreams
I'd learned that they all
Formed our realities of the time
But now I was in awe"

"*Romeo, it's been so long
That we've been navigating
Through the dark and tortuous channels
Of our own acts*

"Weak we have been
Thoughtless, reactive
That in the impulse of our passions
We destroyed the precious gift
To us provided by the divine mercy

"What we've been suffering
Is the consequence of our foolishness
But life never ends
As we are being given new chances
New opportunities

"Romeo, I've been allowed to come
To tell you how happy I am
With the progress of your soul
And the understanding you now have

"Your decision is wise and prudent
Your next task will be hard
But I've been allowed the privilege
To join you in our next sojourn"

"Still paralyzed as a block of wood
I had tears in my eyes
As my heart ached in emotion
As Juliet continued her talk"

"The law is the same for all
And I need to rescue as well
The enormous debt
Created by my horrible act

"I had, however, more choices
As well as time to decide my fate
But what fate is mine
Without being with you?

"Romeo, the law is far-reaching
And we are responsible
For all the results that our acts
Have in anyone, anytime, anywhere

"Many poets have sung hymns
To the love of Romeo and Juliet
Misguiding many young hearts and souls
To imitate our irresponsible acts

"The divine justice will keep us connected
To their suffering
As a result of their senseless acts
We are responsible, Romeo, we are

"The divine love and mercy
Are infinite
And life is an eternal school
With infinite opportunities to learn

"I will be returning as you
Prisoner in a lame body
With little chance to express my soul
But we'll have the opportunity
To observe and meditate

"Not much we'll be able to do
To remediate the results of our acts
In the young hearts in despair
Not much, for a time

"But we will be free at other times
When our bodies rest and the mind sleeps
Our souls will meet
And together again we'll plan

"Twin souls we are
For centuries and centuries we've been
Together, connected evermore
Forever our love will endure

"Your fall is my fall
Your pain is my sorrow
Your smile my light
Your success my happiness

"But weak I remain
With yet so much to learn
In the eternal school of life
In the infinite Universe of love

"Together we will reach the poets
Of now and at all times
To tell them about us
To make them change their songs

"No one may kill for love
As love is ever forgiving
Always creative
Never destructive

"Their verses have influenced many
That in the purity of their ignorance
Have followed our steps
In name of love

"Love is pure and transcends dimensions
Passion is local and limited
Turning us into slaves of our desires
Always selfish, possessive

"Let us help them sing to the world
Hymns to the divine love
Present in us all
As expression of the Creator

"We are indeed these expressions
When divested from our desires
And passions
When realizing our essence

"The real sacrifice for love
Will never contain an act of violence
Either to yourself or somebody else
But patience and resignation"

"Juliet's voice was sweet but firm
As she spoke a halo of light
Brightened her pale face
Presenting to me a beauty
Yet unknown

"Her heart pulsating with each word
Allowed the blood to spill
Reminding me of her pain
My sweet Juliet, not a dream"

ACT VI

Redemption

Verona, circa late seventeenth century

Scene I

<u>Two blue angels</u>

The sunset was especially beautiful
On that autumn day
As the sun sprayed its rays
Over the multicolored leaves

That evening at Villa Bergamo
Was rather unique and agitated
Maids were seen running
From one place to the other

Carriages arriving in a hurry
Bringing anxious, apprehensive people
Expressing grave concerns
Exhibiting respect and sorrow

Doctor Vittorini arrived
Family physician of years
Rushing into the main house
Followed by a court of maids

Master Giulio waiting
Directed the doctor to a chamber
Where his wife, Mistress Giuliana
In her bed agonized in pain

Attended by her maids
The mistress was in great distress
Unable to contain her feelings
In excruciating pain

It had been a long pregnancy
With difficulties from the beginning
And now before them
The pains of labor had begun

The doctor was prompt and caring
In giving her some herbs
To chew and inhale
To soothe her agony, control her pain

There was much to be done
As the hemorrhage was vast
And the baby unborn
Unable to descend and breathe

With his bare hands the doctor
Attempting to turn the baby
And pulling to give him birth
Realized that it was serious
And might have been too late

With a scream that times will remember
Giuliana stopped fighting
And Vittorini through his skills
Delivered the newborn boy

He was blue and not breathing
Requiring all the attention
As the maids held him warmly
Awaiting from a sign from God

The mistress lay unconscious
As the hemorrhage continued
All efforts to revive her
As her breathing could barely be perceived

With all efforts divided
Between the blue boy and the mistress
No one but Giulius perceived
That another child had arrived

It was a girl, and also blue
And without knowing why
Giulius felt connected
He had to save that baby

Words of haste and warning
He held the baby girl in his arms
Cleaning her skin with warm clothes
Crying to God for a miracle

Chaos and turmoil prevailed
As Giuliana in anguish and pain
Screamed again and for the last time
Her eyes looking at Giulius as a plea

As if awaken from a long sleep
The two blue babies
As if rehearsed
Began to cry

The last rays of sun
Entered through the chamber's windows
Suggesting reflection
Requesting a prayer

* * *

Villa Bergamo was somber and calm
A peace that only reality brings
When revealing the transient nature
Of all beings

Pain and sorrow had abated
Through the entire household
As no one could explain
The sudden and mysterious events

Father Totti, as he was called
Was desolate himself
Barely hiding his feelings
Betraying his faith in the Lord

Giulius, however, carried in his heart
The serenity of the wise
The peace of the saints
And the light of his faith

While he contemplated in tears
The pale semblance of his wife
No longer in pain but smiling
A vision appeared to him

He was not seeing with his eyes
Nor listening with his ears
As his beloved Giuliana
So pale and so beautiful
Called his name

"Giulius, do not be sad
A great moment has arrived
A moment of redemption
A moment of great joy"

Giuliana's voice echoed
In her husband's ears
As sweet balsam
Healing his soul

*"We will appear to be apart
Temporarily as it may seem
But with you I'll be all the time
To help you succeed*

*"Our children, now struggling
Are blessings to you and me
So nurture them with your heart
Help them live and thrive*

*"You will be forever blessed
For all efforts and love you give
To the two little blue angels
So frail, defenseless they are*

*"We have known them before
And now you have rejoined
So that love may rebuild the bridges
In the past destroyed by arrogance*

*"I will be with you in this path
Not always sweet and bright
But through your struggles and pain
Bonds of love will arrive*

*"So listen, Giulius, my love
Regardless of what all say
Love our children with all your heart
And be their father and their mother as well"*

His vision began to dissipate
Despite his attempt to cling to it
He opened his eyes and looked at her face
She had that smile, indeed

* * *

A serenade of cries
Followed the procession to the chapel
Where mass was to follow
Ceremonies without end

Giulius observed and followed
Disinterested, amused
All these rehearsed acts
Understanding their futility

"No one brings a word of hope"
He thought to himself
"But gloom and hopelessness
Sorrow and despair

"I feel and realize
That my sweet wife
Is present here and now
Radiant and serene"

Giulius observed all things
Impartial and tolerant
Detached from them
At one with the world

"What is in the casket
If she is next to me?
Her body to be consumed
While her soul endures"

As he let his mind free
Keeping his heart at peace
Giulius was realizing
The miracle of eternal life

The casket descended to her grave
And the priest recited memorized words
Giulius was filled with emotion
"My children," he thought
"My children"

The night extended her dark veil
Over Verona, as Giulius contemplated
The silvery paths that the moon
Reflected in the calm pond

"I will love them
As I love you
And in the name of our love
They will be called
Romeo and Juliet!"

* * *

With all his energies and love
Giulius dedicated his life
To nourishing and protecting
His children, so frail, so lame

He tended to them as special flowers
In a magic and private garden
Using his tears as water
And his love as nourishment

The babies, though struggling
Survived
And Giulius found in them
His motivation to live

He had great affinity
Almost unreal, unexplainable
For little sweet Juliet
That transcended his imagination

As she grew, so did their bonds
And Giulius at times felt jealous
Almost resentful
Of little boy Romeo

Juliet could barely move
The right side of her body
Not able to sit, to crawl
Or walk

Romeo moved quite well
Though he couldn't learn to talk
He seemed somewhere else
Most of the time

The twins seemed to all
To suffice to each other
Almost alienated from the rest
Undemanding despite their difficulties

Giulius perceived that they
Appeared almost resigned
With the impairments they had
Never complaining, never in pain

"Who would the children be"
He pondered
"That from their suffering
Can build their peace?"

Juliet was able to communicate a little
As Romeo was able to ambulate
They complemented each other
Twins they were in body and soul

Their days were simple and pure
Always under Giulius' loving eyes
Happiness one wouldn't call it
But peace they had in their hearts

At night their bodies reposed
And their souls momentarily free
Walked together in joy
Discussing ideas, sharing their love

Prisoners they were at times
Aren't we all?
But aware of their essence they were
Aspiring for great new ventures

They traveled together to lands
Where poets were singing their hearts
Inspiring them in their songs
The divine message of life

Together they had a mission
As difficult as you might think
That love is always creative
Always sublime, never destructive

Every night they traveled together
To the seven confines of earth
Wherever a poem was being written
Wherever a song being composed

Their reality (which one would it be?)
Appeared to most to be sad
By their narrow standards of knowledge
By the blind eyes of religion

But their spirits were being unburdened
From the serious errors of past
In the peaceful prison
Of their lame brains and bodies

But poets when seeking their muse
Opened themselves to inspiration
They could see the couple
Romeo and Juliet in the beauty of their youth

Poets have so much to give
As the entire world waits
To be touched by word of love
Divine love, present in all

Scene II

A dream

As Giulius fell asleep
With his heart in peace
Despite his great sorrow
He felt his body float

Guided by a hand
He knew to be Giuliana's
He was taken back in time
To a time he felt so familiar

He recognized the place
Verona had not changed so much
And he saw himself
Although with different appearance

From noble origin he carried
The arrogance of the unwise
The pride of the small
The violence of the primitive

Uncomfortable he felt with his sight
As he realized who he was
When a teenage girl arrived
Filling his heart with joy

It was his cousin, how beautiful
They had grown together
Fond of each other
Greater friends one couldn't find

She helped him in difficult moments
Comforted him when in pain
Her beautiful voice when she sang
From heaven seemed to come

A sudden change and he was
At the cobblestone streets in Verona
Insulting this young man
Unreceptive to his violence

He felt his body shivering
As he saw Giuliana's image
Pale as an angel
Holding his hand and saying

*"As Thybault you had a choice
To avoid war and discord
However you decided for violence
Instead of promoting peace*

*"As violence always rebounds
Upon oneself
You died in the hands of Romeo
An enemy of many times*

*"Now you are given the blessing
The opportunity to provide
Love instead of hatred
Compassion to overcome all violence*

*"Receive Romeo in your arms
With the love we continue to share
As Juliet returns as well
To help you repair your past"*

As Giulius woke up
Mixed images he had in mind
His sweet Giuliana he remembered
And his babies, the twins

CLOSING CURTAINS

The poet was restless
He had witnessed so much
Reviewed so many things
In time that could not be measured

The image of the couple
Almost children they seemed
Did not leave his mind
Was ingrained in his soul

Walking in the field
Innocently holding hands
They smiled, a deep subtle smile
In their smile was their message

Restlessness moved the poet again
He had understood the message
He had taken into his heart
He knew so well what to do

As he walked by the Thames
Watching the turmoil of people
Duality began to consume him
The struggle between the ego and the self

That evening was the opening
Of the play he worked so hard
In writing, adapting
Producing, rehearsing

All people who mattered in London
Would be attending the show
Critics, nobleman, even the Queen
He heard was planning to come

His poetry he liked
The drama superb
A story of love
With a tragic end

He'd been confident in its success
Enhancing his name
Inflating his pockets
Covering him in fame

And now he had suddenly
A new reality to him revealed
In a flash
Ignore it he could not

The many lives of Romeo
Still fresh in his mind
Culminating with that vision
And their near-angelic smile

But the actors were all ready
For weeks and months memorized
The beautiful lines of his poems
And that tragic message…

The Queen was expected to attend
And he could not disappoint
To give them all what they wanted
Love, lust, drama, and blood

Resolute he walked
Toward the theater house
Confident in himself
Trying to forget what he couldn't

* * *

The theater house was full
Excitement was present everywhere
Electricity was in the air
Expectations of something new

The Queen and her court present
Dignifying the event
Honoring that theater house
The poet observed all in silence

He screened the young faces
And there were so many
Young damsels full of hope
To find their prince one day

Young men with expansive dreams
Of glories and accomplishments
Sensitive, passionate
Eager to sacrifice

Through the curtains the poet looked
And in his mind he began to conceive
"How would they react?"

Throughout the play the suspense lifted
Reactions were easy to feel
Laughter heard when appropriate
At the end all in tears

Deafening was the applause
After a pause of silence
With cheers and bravos
Hats thrown in the air

The poet should have been exulting
Greater success couldn't happen
The Queen signaled to him in approval
All that he'd dreamed, all…

His eyes, however, were looking
For the faces of the young
He needed to see their reaction
Would there be any consequences?

He rejected all invitations
To parties and celebrations
Politely he saluted the public
And almost unperceived
He left

His mind wandered
His thoughts coming from all sides
Created confusion, chaos
The poet hurt inside

He walked without aim
Heavy-hearted and in pain
Not knowing exactly why
What could he have done?

* * *

With the sounds of the city distant
The poet sat down at the riverbank
Letting the moon illuminate his face
He contemplated the stars

He felt detached from all things
Observing the universe pass by
While his mind kept reminding him
Of the young faces of the world

Lying on the sand
He spread his arms and legs
As to reach the four corners of the world
And deeply inhaled
The fresh evening air

A drunkard passed by
And, throwing an empty bottle in the river
Left cursing nature
For his perennial despair

The poet was calm
He felt peace inside
Even knowing so well
That his world was out of control

There was a reason, he pondered
Why all was to him revealed
Why that was to him shown
At this time

He had witnessed all torment
And great suffering
From Hannibal to Romeo
For having ended their own lives

He understood quite well
That what they thought they were ending
Was just the beginning of their suffering
The natural consequence to their acts

Century after century
Life after life
Experience after experience
In the eternal school of life

Enemies of past
Brought together at other times
For a new chance of reconciliation
A new hope for redemption

The poet looked at the river
Flowing inexorably into the sea
That, staying low, humbly waits
To absorb all water it brings

From the brightest star in the sky
Coming in his direction he saw
Romeo and Juliet smiling
Hand in hand they seemed to say

"Poet, the world is yours
You've conquered their ears and eyes
Hearts and souls
Your message is sublime

"Sing your message aloud
As the entire world will listen
Tell them what you know
Tell them what you witnessed

"Poet, your mind has been blessed
With the inspiration of angels
Your words flow as easily as a plume
Enchanting young hearts and minds

"Think of us, poet
Think of us sometimes
Never forgetting where we are
Never forgetting who you are

"Think of us when you feel
The weight of success suffocating
The power of wealth intoxicating
The glory of fame weakening you

"Go, poet, and sing like a bird
Touched by the divine light
Sing life and love
And the realities around

"Don't lead the youth to the error
Of ending what to them is given
As a gift from our Creator
The sacred privilege of life"

The vision evanesced in the air
As the poet's thoughts flew away
To the distant city of Verona
Where they lived as prisoners

Prisoners in their lame bodies
Chained to deficient minds
Free at times, what a blessing
To bring their message to all

Romeo's lives he remembered
Eternal Romeo indeed
Now with his beloved Juliet
Prisoners in flesh, free in spirit

The poet stood up and looked
To the brightest star in the sky
There they were, smiling
With his fingers he cleared the sand
And wrote

"So wise, so young, they say
Never live long"

THE END

Authors' Bios

RICARDO KNOPLOCH PETRILLO was born in 1985. At the time of his passing in 2005 he was a sophomore at Quinnipiac University in Connecticut. He was a member of the Tau Kappa Epsilon Fraternity. He enjoyed music, singing, acting, sports, cooking, and politics.

CLAUDIO R. PETRILLO, MD, has been a practicing physician for thirty-five years. He is the Chairman of the Department of Physical Medicine and Rehabilitation at Norwalk Hospital in Connecticut. He has never written a book either professionally or privately before receiving the writings from his son.

SILVIA KNOPLOCH, MD, has been a practicing physician for twenty-four years. She is a Senior Attending Physician in the Department of Physical Medicine and Rehabilitation at Norwalk Hospital in Connecticut.

For further information, contact: www.eternalbondsoflove.com